Cecil

The Homestead

Embracing observations and reflections on America and Ireland

Cecil

The Homestead

Embracing observations and reflections on America and Ireland

ISBN/EAN: 9783337328627

Printed in Europe, USA, Canada, Australia, Japan

Cover: Foto ©ninafisch / pixelio.de

More available books at **www.hansebooks.com**

THE HOMESTEAD,

EMBRACING

OBSERVATIONS AND REFLECTIONS

ON

AMERICA AND IRELAND,

ON THE WRITER'S RETURN FROM THE UNITED STATES:

WITH

OCCASIONAL POEMS.

By Cecil.

LONDON:

H. E. TRESIDDER, AVE-MARIA-LANE.

1862.

PREFACE.

Some years' residence in the Northern States of America, made the Writer of the HOMESTEAD familiar with the principles on which their Union with the South was based, plainly indicating that a dissolution must be the issue, ancillary to the Pacific States of California, Oregon, &c. &c., becoming, as a third independent Government, the most important of the American Continent !

Those Pacific States possess vast tracts of the richest soil, of the easiest cultivation, a true Eldorado of inexhaustive mineral wealth, with the finest climate in the world ; and, from their natural position, impregnable ; commanding the rich trade of the Eastern Hemisphere, and, by the three hours' railway route of Panama, the commerce of Europe ; to these subjects, the Writer calls the attention of the reader in his first Canto.

The succeeding Cantos, written immediately on the Writer's return to Ireland in 1857, were suggested by the cherished objects of Home scenes and recollections, from which he was occasionally drawn, to note the political and religious aspects of his country, in some passages of which are held up to censure, the purchase system in our Army of a military status, by feather-bed poltroons, to the disgrace of the service— the appointment to magisterial office, of men more anxious to identify themselves with the religious, gypsy abductions, of the Aylward, St. Vincent de Paul system, than to uphold British Law,—as also to the maudlin state patronage, which supplies the most distant parts of the world, and the self-expatriated traitors and French intriguers in America, with legions of Irish Priests, from Colleges and Schools endowed by State grants from England, to extend and support the Church of Pio Nono ; from which are selected Consuls, Attachés, Engineers, &c. &c., nine-tenths of whom obtain foreign appointments as Pio's subjects, to give eclat to a dominancy abroad, which has heretofore been so prolific of Home distractions; and which through British bounty, is cropping up in America those broils, which are now being so happily cultivated there, since the materials for producing such harvests in Ireland, have evaporated before the English Volunteer movement, that has also check-mated the game of the sharper of the " *coup d'etat*," and, through Providence has become the stay of British action and of the peace of Europe, under a first *Minister* of the Crown, who is the pride of the Empire, to whom Ireland is indebted for the appointment of the man, who knew how to place his heel on the inflated impudence of Papal assumptions, to the imbecile arrogance of which, it had become a routine of courtesy to bow for years.

With devoted respect for the Saxon spirit of the man, and with the happiest anticipations from his outspoken policy, to free from Priestly domination the interests of his country—the humble Writer of the following Poem looks, with confiding trust, *to the Right Honourable* SIR ROBERT PEEL, *Baronet, as the Guardian of its Homes and Homesteads.*

CECIL.

THE HOMESTEAD.

CANTO THE FIRST.

Muse, be the Homestead early left my theme,
Ere, of some stranger, it becomes the claim,
As the Demesne, which in the last few years,
Sold to the third proprietor appears.
   Tho' BARRY's merits—lost with the estate—
And name, and family, evaporate,
The Muse, her fee, in lasting lines shall trace,
And claims to memorize her natal place :
The still attractive scenes of early days,
She haply greets again, and here portrays.

   Within a vale, where Leinster's mountains rise,
By woods and streams enclosed, a village lies,
Or rather town—and which for some past years
As Newtown-Barry on the map appears :
Near which an Essex yeoman, years deceas'd,
A Homestead built, on lands by BARRY leas'd;

1

And where the Muse, her inspiration drew
In early youth—and left it early too—
'Midst hills, whose streamlets stealing from some mine,
Thro' sinuous vales, their humble currents twine;
Wending their course through meadow-flats and fens,
Thro' rocky gorges, and thro' wooded glens,
Without a name, the Clody's flow to swell,
Bouncing and noisy as some rural belle!

    This rapid mountain brook, the Clody stream,
Gave to the village heretofore the name
Bunclody—as was graphic of its site,
Where Clody and the Slaney's flows unite—
But when it pass'd to fastuous BARRY's hands,
With its appendages and varied lands,
His sterile house and merits to convey,
Made it the Newtown-Barry of my lay!

    Its market square, an open spacious street,
Where town and country in convergence meet:
Is picturesquely screen'd by woods around;
Which ornament its ev'ry vale and mound!
And midway thro' the street a stream is led,
Where slender plinths of granite hem its bed;
With Lindens—which the carriage ways divide—
Guarding the footway on its northern side,

In military file, whose summer's shade
Makes the short mall a favorite promenade,
'Neath laminated boughs, then thickly set
With astral bloom, like pendent mignionette !
A perfum'd screen in noon-day's heat or showers,
A golden-tassel'd canopy of flowers !
Which every wooing zephyr gently waves,
Stealing the odour from their veiling leaves ;
To win admiring homage, ever new,
Unequall'd in the youthful Muse's view.

When called to mark COLUMBIA's ocean plains,
Her Forests, Rivers, Lakes, and Mountain chains,
On Nature's proudest, widest scale expand,
Each without rival in its class to stand !
Whose rivers—in their tributaries own
Many superior to the Rhine or Rhone—
Flowing in almost fabulous extent,
Each draining in its course a continent !
Where man, for travel-lore, or pleasure led,
Nature before him has her highway spread,
Inviting him to visit those domains
Where her primeval state she still maintains !

Tho' in the forest not much game is found,
In all the rivers tempting sports abound ;

With rod or gun, as sailing in your boat,
Employing each, with pleasure you may float :
And tribes of Bass—the rock, the green and white,
Fast as you bait your hook, voracious bite,
Of salmon size, with luscious muskalunge—
As struggling to get free, they fiercely plunge—
The vigorous captive claims a careful hand,
And angler's skill, to bring his prize to land :
While snipe and duck or other aqueous birds,
Occasionally too, much sport affords.

But, the Prairie, more attractive here,
Presents you game all seasons of the year,
Throughout its ranges and its sinuous streams,
To meet your every wish, prolific teems !
Of the Prairie I had read and heard,
Till it became a quite familiar word ;
And ever lighting up the sportman's thought,
As the rich field where game was to be sought !

And now with friends the pastime I partook,
In shooting deer, and grouse, and various duck ;
But chief the wood or butter-duck I prize,
Plump as a partridge, as the same in size ;

Call'd wood-duck, as the forest she likes best
When brooding, and will there but build her nest :
Where in the hollow of some lofty tree
She safely nides, then bears her progeny
To the next stream, or neighbouring morass,
To nurse them in their pools, and sedgy grass ;
The canvas-back, a larger duck, is deemed
The next in worth—the diver less esteem'd.

The sportsman, to satiety, may here,
For ages yet, pursue a gay career
'Mongst countless herds, and flocks of different game,
With profit too, if such should be his aim.
But passing o'er the various tribes, my pen
The Buffalo but notes, and prairie hen—
Prolific brood, which like their partridge-quail,
Endemic to the clime, can never fail !

I passed some time on this immense plateau,
While BERKLEY here was hunting Buffalo,
But far remote—hundreds of miles at least,
From where he then indulged his Nimrod taste—
Amaz'd and awe-struck, by the scene subdned,
The noting Muse an humbling path pursued,

That led to thoughts of the eternal state ;
The destinies that now on life await :
Bowing before the soul-absorbing sense
Of man's deserts and God's omnipotence !

While passing on from SPRINGFIELD to DU CHIEN,
We must remark the still expanding scene,
And pause again to note with wonder new,
When some Moluscan relic meets the view,
Where still the fossiliferous remains,
Its during type of character retains ;
A record of the past eternal page,
To claim the study of each future age !
Here since this steppe, from its bath of brine,
Rose to the limits of its Andean line ;
When the Moluscan and its Saurian race,
To Mastodon and Mammoth tribes gave place !
These too, in ages past, to disappear,
Succeeded by the Buffalo and Deer :
In those past cycles of Creation's plan,
Ere on the stage of time God usher'd Man !
For immortality design'd and heav'n—
When to his care the rule of earth was given !
And spread those azure curtains o'er these plains,
Incentive to the Muse—where silence reigns—

Remote from Europe's many grating cares,
Which not refining taste or culture spares !
The busy solitudes where adverse men
For prey and traffic crowd the city den !
Here, far from tumult, may the fancy stray
O'er subjects that demand a serious lay.

    Above, a blue ethereal cloudless sky—
Eternal space—the boundless canopy,
Curtains below, around, on every hand,
This Prairie-pampa, truly nam'd " THE GRAND !"
A sea-like plain of undulating grass—
Beyond the vision aided by the glass—
Up to the limits of the Andean chains,
Which hazy distance merges in its plains ;
The heaven-built barrier which separates
The Eastern from the rich Pacific States ;
Whose golden districts the COLUMBIA laves,
Shut in from rowdy mobs and Southern slaves !
Where the prophetic Muse, with vision blest,
Surveys the future Empire of the West ;
And with the British State, Columbia, blent,
Shall spread and crown the Saxon element :
While law and order safety shall propound,
Nor Eastern mobs nor slavery be found !

An Empire in extent, in clime serene,
And rich in rolling plains—as Erin green—
Beyond the rocky mountains plac'd secure,
These great Pacific States, their plans mature ;
Biding the time to seize the coming hour
To raise their golden realms to sov'reign pow'r !
Which a vast sea, and continent more wide,
From Europe's meddling dominance divide ;
Whose trackless wastes and heav'n-built mountains bar
From the invading foot of plundering war !
Another offshoot of the Saxon tree
To bear the fruits of faith and liberty.

To these Columbian views as fancy turns,
My British breast, with glowing interest burns.
With pride of race, for here the Saxon name,
Thro' its extent is ours—its tongue the same !—
And we must ever deprecate the pride
Of bubble rule, which brought us to divide,
Nor could disruption ever intervene,
But thro' the feudal fudge of pomp insane !

When brothers quarrel 'tis a serious case,
With the first love they never may embrace !

Their slightest wounds are hardly to be heal'd,
While to themselves each trace is still revealed !
Nor has America forgotten quite,
What first her Revolution did excite :
And some unpleasant feelings, 'tis confess'd,
She still permits to agitate her breast ;
Promoted by a French and Irish crew,
Whose zeal for Rome and spleen for Waterloo
Train the young Yankee mind, who're taught to scorn
The land of Freedom, where their sires were born !
Throughout the Union, active to foment,
A jealous hate of English sentiment !

Yet still, the rural parts, they fail to lead,
But in the corporations they succeed !
Where Irish O's, and marcid Frenchmen awe,
Thro' rowdy mobs, the ballot-box and law !
Nor in Kilkenny, Drogheda, nor Cork,
Are hurrah blackguards to surpass New York ;
Where tutor, lecturer, or padre plies
His Mission-call, as in our Colonies !

To teach such feelings, and their sphere enlarge,
We train up agents at the Empire's charge,

And chiefly those whom we so educate,
Select from traitors' sons of Ninety-Eight!
Whose French proclivities and Papal zeal
Are school'd for doctors who may preach repeal!
And where such Irish friends may claim a Priest,
For each requir'd we furnish ten at least!
And ship the zealot-surplus of this band,
To every isle, and continent, and land!
And hence the settlements and parts that own
Great Britain's sway, are taught to hold the throne
And institutions of the parent race,
As heretic to Rome and Papal grace!
Which spread the Bible, and uphold the press,
Despite their curses, still to Rome's distress!

And thanks to England's maudlin care, Maynooth
Supplies each foreign school and institute
With pastors still to nurse this British hate,
Which led America to separate!

Yet under Providence, *that* severance leads
To proud results,—it England's influence spreads!
As since Her separation, those State ties
Which bound Her then, when adverse interests rise,
Must be disrupted, as Her vast extent,
Was never destin'd for one government!

For as the principle of sovereign right
Each separate State retains, its acts to light;
New combinations may arise and must,
Each local independence to adjust!

Some States, whose kindred institutions blend,
To a combined and sov'reign union tend;
While others, that more selfish interests court,
Will still the separate policy support;
Progressing to that future state of things
Where interests clash, there separation springs!

'Twixt North and South the Union is a cheat,
Far as we Southern interests estimate,
Tax'd by the North to prop its factory's scheme,
Those play on double stakes, a losing game,
For what is purchased there those doubly pay,
That sword, the tariff, cuts them every way:
Their bills of outlay swell to large amount,
And sinks their produce to a low discount!
Ties agriculture—trammell'd by such bands—
To the sick culture of mere household hands,
By raising labor to the par of rent,
Thro' bounties for the work in factories spent!
The policy, by which free trade is chain'd,
To leave the forests wild, the swamps undrain'd,

The roads, as mud canals, where low the grounds,
And where more elevated, ruts and mounds!

Where legislation is to wealth confin'd,
In something it offends the lib'ral mind,
But where 'tis wholly in the rowdy class,
For safety, liberty, and rights, alas!

Now, to America adieu awhile,
Call'd to return, I hail proud freedom's isle,
Fair England, shield of truth!—but having yet
To greet some friends, I stopp'd near Lafayette—
Ere starting for New York by steam and rail,
While waiting for the Kangaroo to sail,
I was invited by my worthy friend,
On some fine prairie near, a day to spend,
And as he knew where game did much resort,
He'd drive his greys with me, and " *We'd have sport.*"
When to the favorite rendezvous we came,
The distant, dark horizon burst in flame
Of lightnings luminous, and quick as thought,
In zig-zag flittings scarce by vision caught;
The fiery flashes shed their lurid light,
And deaf'ning thunders told their awful might;

In crashing peals, around and overhead,
While the rent clouds, their drenching torrents shed !

Remote from screen, no sheltering covert nigh,
Save what our phaeton might here supply ;
For hours the clouds their teeming urns employed,
But softly tepid, we felt less annoy'd ;
While waned the day, and the incessant rain
With moving sheets of water spread the plain !
Hope now had fled, and ominously late,
We felt 'twas time to make a quick retreat !
Our road a flowing stream—no pleasing view—
With some plank bridges, that would soon float too ;
They could not stand, some totter'd as we pass'd,
'Twas neck or nothing till we reached the last,
'Twas swaying, but we gained the further bank,
When—crash ! the bridge was gone, nor left one plank !

And now but interven'd, the wide spread flow
The ford of Ouio—'tis pronounced weeo—
As we approach'd, its valley was a tide,
And barely light to mark the further side ;
A surging flood, but soon a torrent's force,
With planks and floating beams, would bar our course !

Where much excitement on the passions press,
Reason recedes, not chance is her success !—

Tho' our success on chance alone but stood,

We plung'd the noble steeds into the flood!

Which struggling for their lives to gain the strand,

Tow'd our slight phaeton, thank God! to land;

And gain'd the object of each reckless mind,

While round destruction swept, for God was kind!

Whose Providential hand was prompt to spare

For days of richer grace, a thoughtless pair!

And vivid as I write in mem'ry's glow,

With pearly gratitude my eyelids flow—

O'er the vast catalogue of mercy's rolls,

And links of grace that lead His purchased souls!

But an eternity may only solve

Those mercies, and His love and care evolve,

Which life and immortality inspire,

With faith and hope, that grateful tunes the lyre!

THE HOMESTEAD.

CANTO THE SECOND.

How short the span that realms and friends divides,
Steam bounds the distance over lands and tides!
Obsequious, on the will of man awaits,
And time and space almost annihilates;
When business, love, or pleasure's calls invite,
Prompt and subservient, as Aladdin's sprite,
To waft the tenant of the humblest hearth,
To the most distant climes and scenes of earth!—

   Dear Erin, hail! 'tis but a few days back,
I sported on the banks of Font-du-lac;
Pass'd down Mississippi, and wondering stood
To note Missouri's ever turbid flood,
And placid beauties of Ohio's breast,
Nursing her Queenly city* of the West;
To Hudson's, then to Mersey's busy stream,
Led in the dance of subsultory steam;

     * Cincinnatti is called the Queen of the West.

Thro' each exciting change of scene to find
Health and refreshing hope to buoy the mind—
Nor weary, tho' some little what subdued,
The zest of toil, a pleasing lassitude !—

When won by foreign prospects to resign
The pleasant scenes of home, then priz'd as mine,
In the fond sense, to Bardic feelings due,
I vowed no distant day again to view,
And give the Muse a subject for some lays
Freely, discursive—tho' they should displease—
Untrammell'd in their censure or their praise !
And note, for observation and redress,
Whate'er my country's homes and peace oppress ;
Local or foreign, with unflinching truth,
Amid the fostering shades of early youth,
While prompt to welcome every social spell,
Lighting my visit, ere I'd say farewell !
" And leave some trace upon the sands of time,"
When I should bid adieu to home and rhyme.

Once more the Homestead of my youth I greet,
With throbbing heart, as proud pulsations beat,

In grateful homage to THY sov'reign pow'r,
My GOD, whose mercy spares me to this hour!
O'er youth's gay scenes of mount and dell to stray,
Whilst years of absence shrink to yesterday!
As faithful mem'ry her allegiance brings,
To give a buoyancy to fancy's wings.

But small the scope appears for fancy's range,
In Newtown-barry there is little change ;
The village—once Bunclody, neatly kept—
When made a town the metamorphose wept ;
Losing its name by questionable taste,
For one not so appropriate at least ;
And this was all from BARRY'S grace that flowed—
But nature and position much bestow'd—
He could not prize the landscape's glowing lines,
Rich in the traits creative pow'r combines ;
For too contracted was his narrow mind,
To value gifts inspiring taste refin'd !

My hopes were gay, when call'd to leave this scene,
Nor did a cloud in prospect intervene ;
Life in the distance—as some Alpine height—
View'd from the plains of youth, look'd smooth and bright!

2

Where rock, or chasm, and cataract, and glacier,
As beaming points of interest but appear !
Life's icy path, or sudden adverse tide,
Or early grave, boy-magic sets aside !
Enthusiastic visions fledge the soul
To bear him gaily to the distant goal.

But tho' experience mars the youthful dream,
Still Newtown-barry's aspect seems the same,
As erst in fancy's waking visions clad,
Unchang'd—but oh ! how much had chang'd the lad—
Its woods, its parks, still gay, and shaded rills,
Girt by its amphitheatre of hills ;
Early incentive to Poetic taste,
To be but coldly crush'd, or left to waste !
For no Mæcenas claim'd this fair demesne,
But one emasculate in mind, yet vain
Of the position which his station gave,—
His wish was rather talent to enslave—
Nor science, nor mechanics claim'd regard,
He valued paintings only by the yard !
And Poetry—we need not be severe—
A seraph's lyre would not attract his ear ;
Some younger scions of the lordly tree
Might toy perhaps at wit or poesy ;

But humbler names, tho' God endow'd their mind,
He to some lowly call or trade would bind:
Vain of the order of his worthless line,
He'd all beside to Hindoo class confine!

   This tribute, to the BARRY's merits due,
The Muse suggests, as I her influence woo,
To lead me with th' historic page once more,
Among those early paths I've trod before:
And those dear seats of study where I've read,
And only clos'd the book when light had fled:
While busy recollections urge a claim
To give their early impress to my theme,
The truthful Muse her humble verses sings,
And tribute to home scenes her effort brings;
Where warm pulsations first my boyhood fir'd,
And all the Patriot in my breast inspir'd,
With love of Britain and the Saxon sway,
That prompt my aspirations from that day:
In politics, in faith, or travelled bourn,
And still responsive beat on my return.

   High throbs the pulse, nor may the patriot soul
The noble swellings of the heart control,

While proudly fires the eye, where glorious deeds
Illume the page of Britain, as he reads
What stars have rose and set her worth to swell ;
How Sidneys, Falklands, Mackeys, Gardiners fell !
True Christian heros who resign'd their breath—
In duty—on her battlefields to death !
How FRANKLIN sought the Pole, as CLAPPERTON
And PARK, for science, made the torrid zone
Their sphere of action—more repelling none—
Whose Saxon nerve Great Britain's flag unfurl'd,
To plant it on the limits of the world !
And made each field of enterprize their tomb,
Where nature spreads her pall of death and gloom !
In latitudes of earth before unknown,
Won for the empire and the British Throne :
And in the battlefield of life's career,
Their names enroll'd with England's fame appear.
Thus FRANKLIN, with his brave compatriots, flies,
At Britain's call, to win her frozen prize ;
And, martyr to his zeal and duty, dies !
She lost another NELSON in that son,
To mourn his fate where nothing could be done !
But where she could have render'd aid, and save
Her host of heros from the Indian grave

Of Moslem massacre! alas, oh Muse!
None may her Horse-Guards' policy excuse;
Where wealth not merit, family not worth,
Its patronage has heretofore call'd forth;
Where red-tape-rule the Empire's interest mocks
To trammel NELSONS or some Havelocks!

Muse, with contempt and destestation brand,
The system that on such routine would stand;
Which since the reign of Anne has prov'd a bar
To England's arms, in science and in war;
While Kepple prototypes, or Elphinstons,
Some ass of honor led her lion sons!—

The soldier's friend, himself the soldier true!—
And none superior witness'd Waterloo—
The hero diplomat and Christian friend,
Whose deeds from Herat to Lahore extend!
Whose Saxon soul and energies untired,
His noble band with kindred impulse fir'd,
And patriot zeal, whose feats of high renown
Secur'd the Indian Empire to our Crown—
By super-human toils he clos'd the strife—
Then on his country's altar pour'd his life!

'Twas thus that HAVELOCK devoted fell ;
He scorn'ed to play the Horse-Guard game, to sell,
Tho' long o'erlook'd, oh shame ! he still remain'd
And had to purchase—till he rank attain'd—
From poltroons, who but traded to acquire
A Company, to sell it, and retire ;
Holding a rank of service and repute,
For pocketing their stakes, and pay to boot ! —

This dastard's object and this sharper's game,
To play at soldiers, should be mark'd for shame ;
That embryo heros to their call might press,
Nor speculating puppies bar success !—
Where mess-room dandies, or some noble pet,
The honorary medal sometimes get ;
As titles, rent-rolls also give the cue,
Where such may gaily dangle on a few ;
By which a modest vanity is fed ;
Meeds of some charge the wearers never led !
Alas for merit ! where such plea obtains
Distinctions which the service only stains.

A NELSON, MOORE, or HAVELOCK may crown
The names of Britain with a world's renown,

To fall neglected, sacrificed, or die
Exhausted by their toils in victory!
But England's routine may o'erlook the worth,
That wins her Empire over seas and earth:
While seizing still their conquests as her prize,
Her nobles to such merits close their eyes;
With lordly whig or tory nonchalance,
Leave such mean cares to Yankee-land or France!
The Heav'n inspir'd, if humble, of their land,
While living, their attentions can't command;
'Tis only when in death such stars descend,
And every heart is bleeding, they commend!
Yet they are ever prompt to smirk and stoop,
To the French drum-boy who may gain a troop!
And to their drawing-room, in proud Saint James',
Lead such to squire their daughters and their dames;
But relegate to toil and chill neglect,
The English yeoman from their clique select:
As in their feudal-feelings of conceit,
They may not home-born merit tolerate
To claim a hope of entree to their camp—
The effete gothems of this German stamp—
But which is open to admit the spawn,
The spurious of the ermine or the lawn!

Which never fails thro' some kind pirouette,
To renovate a senile coronet:
For the sanhedrim councils of the seers,
To give new hybrid life to Alfred's Peers!

Some great authorities on nature's laws,
Who from effects so nicely trace the cause,
Inform us Princes often spring from slaves,
And bastard births give heros, wits and Braves!
And three Nap...ns in this point of view,
Prove that the inference is somewhat true!
The first was great—the second scarce was tried—
Louisa's secretary's son—he early died;
But Verheul's son,—he whom Hor...se nurst,
Is held by many equal to the first;
And, as the third stands out, in bold relief,
A per...d, mur...ing, plotting, scribbling chief!
A sort of Jehu for the welcome feat,
The Bourbon-Ahabs to exterminate;
But his chief Mission-call appears to be,
The demolition of the Papacy!

The dear Republic which he swore to guard,
Met from his truth, its merited reward!

His crimson grape-feast of the *coup d'etat*,
Made France sing " Vive l'Empereur —hurrah !"
While of French freedom !—that utopian theme —
He sent to Hades hosts of souls to dream !

French necks and chains have ever been allied,
Inviting still some despot to bestride ;
To drive and spur them to manubial raids,
For which gay La-Belle-France her hosts brigades.
Give France some Attilla to lead her Huns,
And she'll enjoy the murder of her sons !—
The desecration of her social ties,
While freedom from her restless orders flies !
Where conscript helots, food for lance and ball,
To crown some base-born Nadir-shah, must fall !
And charity may own such monkey train,
Suit well for sacrifice where tyrants reign !—
Who even their Church and Pope would give as fee,
To be the winner in some dear melee ;
Their Frog-broth and their ruffles too forego
To spread, on neighbouring lands, their bones as snow,
For bon-bon *Lodis* or a *Marengo !*
Freedom, faith, morals, men may prize, but then
French souls are vanities—save one in ten—

With France their deity, thro' every phase,
The love of La-Belle-France each action sways :
Republicans, Napoleonists, Bourbons,
Or Orleanists, they worship France as sons ;
At home, abroad, thro' every rank and sphere,
Juggler and pauper rivals here the Peer !—
Unlike the Irish celt—not Priest can sway,
Nor party win them Empire to betray !
In all French normal institutes the State
Requires for action, merit must compete,
And practical test theoretic rules,
Thro' all the routine of her public schools !
The embryo Marshal, from his earliest teens,
Is duly train'd for military scenes :
As for diplomacy—the statesman's part—
Some infant Talleyrand is taught the art :
And each cadet, attache, engineer,
Must be prepared to rival his compeer !
Hence their address, in war or treaty, shewn :
To such Coimbras, Kybers are unknown !
Nor would be sent the *honorable* fool
To play the English feat of a Cabul !
For leaders of French councils, or French hordes,
Are skill'd to use their wit, as well as swords.

Here, humbled, from the tact of France I turn,
And feel with shame my British brow to burn;
In England, wealth, not worth, obtains the grade,
As military rank is stock in trade ;
And where some mamma's pets may cut a dash
A year or two, by donning sword and sash,
To buy a company, and then retire,—
For life the Captain! as he doffs the squire !

Buy Horse-Guards' scrip—it is the legal stamp
For hero-Captains—Messieurs Dolt and Scamp !—
And for each hundred of your safe out-lay,
You take some thirty pounds per cent as pay—
Quite free from risk, from danger too exempt !
A speculation that a Jew might tempt,
And tho' a Falstaff, you may mount the stairs
To act some new Cabul, or Buenos-Ayres !
But rather purchase to a Captain's claim,
And then sell out—the usual trading game—
Holding a military rank for life,
To make some conquest as the Captain's wife !
Saving your out-lay and a dastard's shame,
And, without risk, a military fame !

What numbers of this poltroon class we meet,
Lounging the parks, or strutting thro' the street ;

And redolent of civet, musk or nard,
For picnic campaigns whisker'd as a pard,
To taunt the man of worth, by action steel'd,
Who stood the charges of the Battle-field !
And to his blood and merits, added gold
To gain a rank so many dastards hold !

The ardent youth, whose taste and talents blend,
The interests of the Empire to extend :
May, in his progress, seek the worthy aim
Of independence and an honor'd name ;
Whose love of country patriot feeling warms,
And science brings to aid his deeds in arms ;
When fully for his call the youth is taught,
Perhaps the first commission should be bought,—
Open to all who choose the path of wars,
When qualified and true competitors !—
An entrance-fee ! but then each other step,
Merit, and only merit, henceforth, get !
But to sell out, a Medean law should stop,
And close such door from every dastard fop !
The soldier from the ranks, must always be
Approv'd, whose duties long have paid his fee !

'Tis love of country bids the Muse unveil
An evil which 'tis requisite to heal;
Wakeful, the Empire's interests should not wane
In growth and glory, nor a fungus stain!
And what excision needs, she may not spare,
Where England's honor claims her proudest care.

Proud of my country, rais'd by Empire's ties
To share in Britain's glorious destinies;
Whose ark of freedom still securely rides
Above those Revolutionary tides,
Which burst their barriers in forty-eight—
Swamping the rule of each despotic State—
Our happy Britain stood secure alone,
To rule the waves that totter'd every throne;
By special Providence shut in and blest,
Calmly reposing in exalted rest!

In ev'ry climate, and thro' ev'ry age,
Of savage manhood, or of sainted sage,
The love ef country in the human breast,
Swells with devotion, not to be repress'd.
Health, station, offspring, partner we resign;
But still our country round the heart-strings twine!
The most tenacious of all earthly ties,
Which but relaxes when the Patriot dies!

In the last pulse of life !—that awful goal,
As starts into eternity the soul—
When to time's objects closing was the eye,
Then, was not, "oh! my country," a last sigh?
Nor heathen knight, nor consul-chief as brave
To death devoted, that the Curtius' grave,
To save their State, may to the zeal aspire
Of him who in the POLE forgot the sire!
And in this sensibility of heart,
A lovely heroine performs her part,
The cheerful victim to her sire's success,
Dies self devoted, with the sweet address,
"Thank God, by you our country is set free,
My father, keep your vow! think not of me."
And need we name the high prophetic saint,
Whose love of country lives in that sweet plaint,
He penn'd on Cheber's banks, with streaming eyes,
Naming his captive land life's dearest prize.

 'Tis kindred feeling makes my breast expand,
As I revisit thee, my native land—
So long abandon'd to the papal heel,
To Demagogues, and treason's hope, "repeal"—
To find thee true to faith and Empire's ties,
And yet repressing Rome's conspiracies,

Thro' those O'Brawlers in her tethers led,
And Smith O'Bubbles of some cabbage-bed !

There's something truly graphic in the O,
Pregnant of Irish vanity and show ;
A talismanic patent for the trade
Of major for a bagnio or brigade !—
That magic circle constitutes each loon,
Milesian chief and cousin to the moon.—
The Dyle from Holland, set on Irish soil,
Becomes a genuine Paddy in O'Doyle ;
As the Dutch Hagan too becomes the same,
By that prefix of nought before his name !
The Farrel, come from Lyons, or Savoy
The Father-land, converted by that toy,
Prays an O'Farrel, happy with his beads,
And, proud as Punch, the great big O parades
As colonel of O'Pats, true church police,
And Saxon's hearty foes—for England's peace—
And when again the lads of *Trinity*
Dare joke, and give pretext for a melee,
Their Saxon houses each in the affair,
As Egypt once, may have to mourn an heir !

This pious corps—to the O'leader thanks—
Can bear no heretic to taint their ranks ;

Yet Saxon Higgins, Beckets, Mores, or Grey,
When they adopt the beads and O they may !
As ev'ry Norman Fitz, or Saxon Fane,
Tho' of the English stock, admixt with Dane,
Soon as the Irish beads and O inflate,
They feel for British rule their church's hate.
As when the Teuton to the mass has knelt,
His dogged zeal for Rome exceeds the Celt !
And, what not bigotry, his pride sustains
To hold him in traditionary chains !
For tho' a Norman-Saxon by his blood—
The family is one, a brotherhood—
And born a son of Britain, now his hope
Of Earth or Heav'n concentres in his Pope !
With hate of England, and the more intense,
The more she yields—the Irish incidence—
Nor may his heart, with patriot cares, expand,
In the proud feelings due to freedom's land ;
The Empire pride, that noblest bosoms swells,
His papal pupilage with care repels ;
The Circean cup of church has chang'd the man
Into an insect of the Vatican !
Whose only buzz is now Saint Peter's See,
And the priest-king of catholicity ;

Whose universal sceptre is his theme
In waking visions, as in sleep his dream !—

'Tis thus tho' Saxon blood and names pervade
Most Irish families, of ev'ry grade,
Some disavow their race, a marcid few,
More celtish than the Celt, a brawling crew,
Tutor'd for demagogues in Jesuit schools,
Who, to advance such interest, hold them tools !
This lazar troop—an ultramontane corps,
Whose yearly freaks kept Ireland in a roar,
Are dwindling to a most amusing faction,
And happily sporadic in their action,
Noisy, indeed, but in a new vocation,
For poorhouse patronage, or Corporation
Merg'd in the blatant family of O's,
A mark that as Gehazi's merit shews !

Man came from nothing, as some lyrists sing,
And from this nothing, Irish patriots spring
To notoriety, these O's the mark ;
Which one Milesius stole from Noah's Ark :
And dropping some in Spain, from thence he flew
To Connaught, and dropt there O's don't-no-who !

3

And Erin budded green ! till ev'ry thing,
Ev'n names, grew emerald in this magic ring !
Rowes, Reynolds,Redmonds, Carrolls, Hagens,Hughes—
Who're just as much of Irish as Hindoos !—
Prefixt the O which gave them claims to rave
Of freemen's rights, while each the self-sold slave
To foreign trammels, body, mind, and soul ;
The mere appendants to the papal stole,
And holding all men foes, and mark for steel,
Who to their idols would refuse to kneel !—
Yet from this class of men, some statesmen draw
Their tools to work in Ireland English Law ;
Handing the Bar, the Bench, and Britons' rights,
To the surveillance of Rome's sbirri knights !
Who sought to disintegrate, by their wiles,
The social ties, that wed the British Isles !

     The Union to preserve was made a plea,
To buy the beagles who were prompt to bay
Against the unity, with Patriot thought
Of being noisy only to be bought :
A Buonaparte such merits would have paid,
With better tact—a patent fusillade—
Nor could the measure traitors disunite,
They're hopeless in the hope their rows excite !

The British Isles a Providence had knit
Indissolubly, nor was needed Pitt!
His too officious meddling help'd to throw
Some stepstones in the stream that mar its flow,
Where roots of treason cling around their base,
And the mob-mud secures their resting place!
His State endowments for a foreign creed,
Becomes a scourge ; and Britain's peace must bleed.

When statesmen principle and manhood lack,
Expediency their cowardice must quack ;
Shrinking from spectres which their fears array—
The vague phantasma of some Jesuit's play—
In mawkish courtesy they try to cloak
Those fears, which still new treasons but evoke !
Where anile spinsters privileg'd preside
O'er state affairs, by fief of feudal pride,
To flirt in matron dotage, and coquette
With effete quidnuncs of another set ;
And gothem beaus consult with tory prudes,
How best to fondle ultramontane broods ;
They must but deprecate their fearful gains
In having hatch'd to life such *Frankensteins !*

My country's freedom I would fain uphold,
Sacred from helots, who themselves have sold :

And, with disgust abhorrent, must detest
Those who, for ultramontane ends, would wrest
The laws and justice—with unblushing face
To screen some cleric Ravaillac of peace—
Who have not manhood, and no shame controls,
But in their porcine merits wrap their souls!

   Alas! that rulers such men elevate
On seats of justice to adjudicate;
Men slaves to despotism from their birth—
Whose faith would in such doctrines trammel earth—
Who close their eyes to truth, and will not read
The glaring lessons of their fallen creed;
Whose shattered institutions fill the page
Of the recording Angel of the age:
In lines refulgent, warning all to fly;
" Come out of her, my people, ere ye die."

   But strong delusion seems to warp their sense,
All scripture teaching gives such men offence:
They stone its readers and its texts besmear,
Where posted for instruction, safe from fear;
Whose teachers cheer them as their creed befits,
And if arraign'd by Law, the Bench acquits!

   The heathen Roman, to his duties true,
The Magisterial sword of justice drew

Upon his sons, nor sought to stay the stroke,
But let them suffer by the laws they broke ;
Nor let the father's feelings interfere
To veil their guilt and stain the curule chair !
In justice stern, he won a high repute ;
But such men now Rome's interests would not suit.
Our Paddy magistrates, with other aim,
From mother-church seek their historic name ;
In base subservience, here, they will devise,
The action of the Laws to neutralize ;
When they some Rev'rend culprit wish to free,
To do the feat, and 'stablish Bigotry,
They wash him in some suds of chican'ry :
And by this ultramontane process *Lave*
le aders in Priestly broils, when Laws they brave !
From districts bless'd by such a state of Law,
Peace, property, and progress must withdraw :
And *the wild justice of revenge*, may plead
To murder, while their press condones the deed !
Where Jurats of such worth for notice prays,
Muse, hold them up to shame their patron's gaze,
While infamy a bleeding trace may plough,
And furrow with disgrace each helot's brow ! —

I love my country—with a love intense—
And constitution, freedom's true defence ;
And as a British subject, proudly stand
For England's Laws and rights, for this fair land,
Won by our sires' good swords, and Britons true,
Whom providence commission'd to subdue,
And plant the liberty that warm'd their breast
On ev'ry soil their conquering footsteps prest ;
While handmaid to their worth, their language ran,
Teaching those doctrines that ennoble man.
And despotism fell, and heathen rights,
Before the page of truth, that freedom lights ;
The Book of God—the living word revealed—
To guide the simple, which the Lamb unseal'd,
That they who read, may run the heav'nly road,
Free from all imposts on the way to God.

   Then shrines of saints and meretricious tolls,
Those taxes of a Church's trade in souls,
Rome carried oft, appall'd by England's light—
The Gospel mission that illumed Her might—
Till under Pusey veils her Monks she set
In College chairs to teach the cabinet ;
Then, thro' her pupils moved, who now evoke
Her trappings, in the Pusey incense smoke,

Which clouds the Altars acolytes now rise,
In the eclipse for new idolatries!
Wooing the Horse-Guards' aid, which it concedes,
That where her monks the wafer host parades,
The soldier's homage should attend such tricks,
And bow the British arms before the Pix!
Ah! since this lapse of faith in hapless hour,
The step has been a curse to England's pow'r;
While cordons of police around are thrown,
To honor those who worship wood and stone!
Whose faith but kneels to God, they now neglect,
And leave the tutor'd mobs to disrespect,
When a La——le may lead, or Petcherine,
Who to the flames our Bibles may consign;
As public bonfires for the rabble's sport,
Within the very precincts of the court!

In India, as in Ireland, we are taught
To feel what such a policy has brought:
Here, we must deprecate the fearful cost,
Famines and pestilence our land exhaust:
As there, whole massacres and lust pursue
Our patronage of Brahma and Vishnu!
Nor less our home with India's ills must mix,
And flow our cup for worshipping the Pix;

As where, Belshazzar-like, we God insult,
Cawnpores or *Scullabogues* are the result !
Nor parents' rights may claim the care of law,
Where combin'd clubs its actions overawe ;
And when the Aylwards kidnap to recruit
The ranks of waning Rome, they win their suit :
As counsel pleads and justices decree
To trample Law, their license must be free
Alike from censure, as from penalty.
While deputations on their Levees wait,
To laud such deeds, and corporations fete !
What Rome requires—however base the deed—
Such sympathies will compass for its need !—

Yet still the lay and cleric stays of Mass
Sent from her training schools—a numerous class—
At Britain's cost abroad, are found to fail;
'Tis but where England rules, their wiles avail :
In every other land they are despis'd,
While here their mobs the laws have neutraliz'd !
And stricken Rome her various orders pours
On Britain's bounteous soil, in teeming scores
Of matron troops, and to receive the flood,
Retreats are builded for each sisterhood :

Whom England and her colonies embrace,
As papal governments refuse them place.
And where the Padre's manse and schools abound,
The palace too for Lady Nuns is found ;
Who, National, as convent schools, employ,
The youth of other churches to decoy,
As privileg'd by State, in latent hope,
To win our population for their Pope !

Now call'd to muezzins by convent chimes,
To morning, noon, and evening pantomimes ;
Hasting from north and south, from west and east,
Crowds come to pray and pay—a troupe to feast
Of foreign actors, in some jubilee !—
Two-pence, the floor ; and six, the gallery ;
While missal, rosary, lustration feats,
The Jesuit-corps-dramatic explicates ;
Deck'd out in church theatric costume gay,
To suit the phases of the parts they play !
While all the treasures that the cross convey'd,
These harlequins have made a stock in trade,
Of which are sold some counterfeits to man—
Free grace is treason to the papal plan —

As *Agnus-Deis*, scapulars, and bones,
And teeth of devotees and decade stones,
Wafers and chrysms, and nails, and bottled blood,
And of the cross—in tons—true chips of wood,
As sure medicaments for ev'ry care
To which the sinful race of man is heir:
And humbly sought, they wondrous virtues shed,
To suit the dying reprobate, or dead !
And from each path of life to chase away,
Fairies and demons—*when the price we pay !*—

Yet 'spite of all these agents and the aid,
That Pusey statesmen grant, their prospects fade ;
The Babylon they woo, to fall, is doom'd,
The gulf now yawns where she must sink entomb'd ;
And monarchs long her slaves, now rise and wait
To mock her wailings, in her hour of fate !
That fate in view I hail, when she must sup—
And to the dregs exhaust—the double cup
Of the destruction of her mitred pow'r
And kingly crown !—now verging to the hour—
When as the millstone, buried in the wave,
Her record must be lost, nor found her grave !

When from the Tarpeian rock her monk-rais'd throne—
And as Saint Peter's blasphemously shewn—
Shall to its base by Angel hands be hurl'd
In ocean's depth, no more to curse the world!
To sink for ever in the gulphing flood—
Charg'd with the Church's tears and Martyrs' blood!

The prelude echoes of Waldensian cheers
Even now are booming in the Muse's ears;
Nor more their matron's wail, nor maiden's shriek,
Borne on the gale shall blench the conscious cheek!
But rather thundering Alleluias rise
To shake the Alps, in homage to the skies!
Call'd from the Altar where they've rested long,
On Rome's downfall to swell the Church's song.

Muse! let me hail prospectively their praise,
And, to their Anthems, tune my humble lays.

THE HOMESTEAD.

IN the apostacy of twenty-nine,
When Whig and Tory, Laic and Divine,
Thy rulers, Britain, then, their trust forswore,
And prince, and peer, and prelate, bow'd before
The papal shrine, and took its mystic brand !
Still firmly stood the yeomen of thy land,
To battle in the truth for victory,
Nor then, nor yet, to Babel bow'd their knee ;
Assur'd, thro' Providence, that England yet
Would leave the renegades with Rome to set !

And tho' to sixty-six the index tends,
And rapidly her tottering pow'r descends,
Each Pusey peer her sinking cause defends!

Austria, her bigots in our councils sees,
As Rome and Tuscany, their Normanbys;
A dilletanti *class*, who strain their jaws,
In trying to pronounce their rrs as aaws.——
As in our pulpits too, such tones are bay'd,
Where poodles of this hybrid mix have stray'd—
And in our senates, for Diana Great,
Their Pio Nono, row on row create!
Where some mass Knight, or tinpot Baronet,
For despotism's hope, a Copley pet,
Have *brush'd* their pathway to the coronet,
By the mob method plan, a mode most sure
To open to a titled name the door!
As if you've kin a Priest or cenobite,
Train'd at May——th to libel, scold, and fight,
In C——'s or M'H——le's pythonic phrase,
Place and Nobility must crown your days!
You've only but to learn to spout and fume,
Be in a passion, or a rage assume,
At England's heresy and tyrant reign;—
Your relatives an audience will obtain,

And crowds to cheer you Erin's Patriot son—
Then get some Landlords shot, your title's won,
If such small victims for your country's good,
Are of the ruling party's clique and blood,
'Tis' certain !—to the ministry convey
The hint, your friends all ferment will allay,
And still their apprehensions and their fear,
Just for the *vacant wig, and make you peer,*
With some few chairmanships for friends you know
As serfs to Rome ! and you're gazetted so !

This happy plan that alienates true friends,
The Demagogue's and Rebel's hope extends ;
And modern statesmen, to this programme bow,
Whose faith and honour, foggy as their vow,
Evaporate before the tutor'd mob,
The Church prepares to work some Jesuit job !
And then the noonday murderer may smile
At justice, and may travel thro' the Isle,
With welcome to partake the board and bed
Of those who by insulted Law are fed !
Where the assassin and his haunts are known
By pious pastors privileg'd alone,
To lampoon law and ev'ry breach condone !

While their complicity, by reticence,
Involves them in the guilt of each offence :
Holding the Laws of England in contempt,—
As subject to a foreign head exempt,—
And thus the Church, by patented device,
Still wins her suit, thro' rulers' cowardice !
As in the circle she adjusts so well,
For years she's had some trusty sentinel ;
To whom was known, of State, each aim and plan,
Thro' wife or mistress, for the Vatican !

First WILMOT HORTON, Rome's true secret son,
For Jesuit counsel a position won ;
And ever since a footing it maintains :
Holding of cabinets sometimes the reins,
When ev'ry institution of the land
Is handed over to an alien band ;
And army, law, police, and finance too,
Crouches before some Priestly bug-a-boo !

When for the Empire's peace, potato-blight
Struck thousands down, and millions put to flight,
And P—ts and Demagogues in wildering dread,
Forsook the rebel's trade, while villains fled ;

The dalliance of our anile chiefs renew'd
The treasons, which a Providence subdued !
Nursing new leaders with official sops,
Full soon their dotage rais'd more noxious crops,
The curse of Empire's peace ! and alien tares
Spring up as patronage the soil prepares !—

England, thy yeoman still thy hope sustains,
'Tis due to him that yet thy pow'r remains !
Some Nobles British principles belie—
Cowards and traitors to thy destiny !
As where they mawkish condescension pay
To hostile creed, thier specious favors stray ;
Which, party hypocrites of rank extend
To England's foes, while they insult the friend !

'Tis ominous of evil, tempting fate,
Where courtesies and treasons osculate ;
When to each feint, or purpose, these avow,
Thro' lust or guile for conscience, those allow !
As principle to politesse will yield,
When statesmen have not love of truth for shield :
Then ev'ry step, in their politic dance,
Leads off to France thro' Rome, or Rome thro' France ;

And wins a snuff box, or a carious tooth,
Some sainted knave's, a relic thro' Maynooth :
But gilt and bless'd, by Pio Nono given,
Will pass the Countess and her Lord to heav'n.

The Whig or Tory, Knight or Lord, half atheis'
Was ever most obsequious to the Papist ;
Nor may we ascertain in statesmen's school,
Whether Napoleon, or the Pope should rule ;
They kiss the beads in homage, or look pale,
As frowns the Dutchman, or to soothe M'H...le ;
Or he, the Legate, here by Pio sent,
The brawling Irish movements to foment ;
Whose periodic edicts spread our walls
In proclamations, or with pastorals ;
Harmonic with the ultramontane growl
Of the puff-adder in Saint Jarlath's cowl ;
Who sibilant and restless in his cage,
Denounces Britain still in Priestly rage,
With the big Doctor of the pen, than whom,
Not Proteus could so many shapes assume !
Priest, chemical professor, electrician,
Philologist and weekly politician ;

4

And the Adonis, as grave rumour tells,
Of those amours, which rear'd confessionals !
Who haply since his Doctorate he won—
And left the arms of sparkling Mrs ———— !
Employs his pen and virtues in the task,
Our English peccadillos to unmask.

Who has not noticed, where rank puddles flow,
Some monster weeds in rank luxuriance grow,
A miasmatic atmosphere to spread
Where febrile influence is largely fed ?
Thus from a seminary tank of state,
Where aliens' enmity we cultivate,
A putid order oozes, to entail
Those treason fevers in the Commonweal,
Which Reverend Doctors, in their holy spite,
By weekly doses constantly excite :
Which thro' the rabid medium they diffuse
Of some low print—the oracle of stews—
A telegraph for burglar-clubs or spies,
And which assassins chiefly patronize.

Is there a moral or politic evil,
Achiev'd by demon, or inspired by devil,

To curse mankind, and progress upon earth ?
To England's agents is ascrib'd its birth !
For ever busy in new complications
To mar Saint Peter's throne and Papal nations :
As where the priestly rule, its freedom rears,
There England with Her Bible interferes !
The hated cause of those pythonic throes
Of C...l which his ev'ry letter shews ;
And may we note the fact, Lord Pam...ton,
To whom are groan'd whole columns, thinks them fun.
Ah ! had his Lordship tried to be discreet,
And knelt attentive at the Doctor's feet,
He had been taught to master every part   .
Of Europe's policy, with happiest art !—
All continental schemes and mysteries,
And ev'n the secrets of the Tuilleries !—
But then my Lord, neglecting this small cost,
The golden opportunity has lost !
Nor other knows, since Baalim's gifted ass,
Except the Doctor, what has come to pass !
Earth's, Heaven's most secret counsels it appears
Some wizard whispers in the Doctor's ears ;

By him we learn, when war in heav'n began,
'Twas English agents arm'd the divan ;

As seizing too the moment to deceive,
When the first slumber clos'd the eyes of Eve;
'Twas England prompted Satan to draw near,
And told him what to whisper in her ear;
And by his logic, it is also plain,
That England made a fratricide of Cain!
And cursed Britain and her Bible-faith,
Seems likely now to haste the Doctor's death,
And that asmodean spouse, his church, so pure,
With Pio Nono, her prince accoucheur;
Whose rare obstetric skill achiev'd the feat
Of bringing Mary forth, full grown, immaculate!
But in his somersault of joy broke down,
And compromis'd his mitre and his crown!
Prostrate and floundering since his feat, he lies
Helpless, and whom no friendly hand may rise;
And 'mongst the happy witnesses, there's none
More smiling than the Church's eldest son,
Louis Napoleon, once the Doctor's pet,
Till his vaticinations, Nap upset,
Then disappointment paled his Irish hope,
Nor sack'd was London, nor was help'd the Pope,
And French invasion, late the Doctor's rod,
To scourge base Albion when he chose to nod,

Has prov'd a myth, the mere ideal dishes,
His dreams supplied, to feast his loyal wishes !
Quite disappointed in the Buonaparte,
He casts the B...d's interests from his heart,
Ireland disowns him now, and all good Pats
Wish him at Saint Helena, with the rats !
And Doctor-rhapsodists in rage may chafe,
As Britain's pow'r expands—'tis rooted safe !—

France years ago, now Austria must in turn,
Howe'er reluctant, Priestly influence spurn :
Only in Ireland now and fallen Spain,
Are helots found to wear the bigot's chain ;
In ev'ry other country, have been broke
The galling trammels of the Papal yoke,
The hateful chain whose ever grating chinks
To discord led, till freedom snapt the links !
And which to join and gild, again to bind,
For ultramontane ends, the British mind ;
The Colleges, the Bench, and Boards combine
To furnish men to work out this design. ·
Some tools are got, of the big O'Baloon,
Some by the flag of a long tried platoon !

A phalanx true to its imperial dyes,
Whose faith and duty fitly harmonize ;
Devoted to the Empire's weal, in truth
With the affection trusting as a Ruth ;
But much too fond of *titled rank*, they stoop
For scions of this class, to lead their troop,
Whose tutors are the papal covert stay,
And thus, great Britain's interests, these betray !

While Britain kept herself distinct, retir'd,
Aloof from idol creeds, she stood admir'd,
Safe from the complications which have rent
The pie-bald kingdoms of the continent,
Sacred to fame, beneath the sure defence
Of the protecting hand of Providence,
That made her walls of waves, more safe than brass,
Which pride's invading feet should never pass ;
Nor danger but from lapse of faith could rise,
When Ahaz-like, her court would patronize
The idol-altars, and those heathen shrines,
Which late are rais'd by Oxford-taught divines :
To whom the magnates of the land consign
Their heirs ! whose Pusey teachings undermine
Their faith and policy : and hence we see
For years the bar to British unity !

Counsel at discord, principle and men,
Amid the hissing of the wildering den,
Misnam'd a senate, now a viperous crew,
From which alone has long been kept the Jew!—
Obnoxious from some reformation's taint,
Not owning goddess, idol-god, or saint!—
While there the infidel, or social friend,
May in the care of Christian interests blend,
With ALIENS, who a foreign monarch own,
And with new deities invest God's throne!
Yes! with the Deity they dare to sport,
When such amusement suits the Papal Court;
And with a bold, unblushing brow assume
The church of Christ *must* be its church of Rome!

'Tis on this postulatum has been built,
The pow'r that human blood in torrents spilt,
And plac'd in despot's hands a sceptre rod,
To paralyze the decalogue of God!
As " hear the church" all controversy clos'd;
A fiat which the Deity depos'd.

When into Moses' hands the Law was giv'n—
The Decalogue—inscrib'd in stone from Heav'n,

Fity no POPE, nor *Wiseman* there, to lend
His aid, the *second* and the *tenth* to mend,
And spare the blunders of the Deity,
Before the records met the public eye !
Which since took so much labour to undo,
That to expunge and mould the tenth to two ;
Seemly to keep the number, as enroll'd
But veil'd to sight, while to the ear as dol'd !
'Tis a strange privilege, for man or gnome
To teach Omnipotence, yet plastic Rome,
When gods and goddessess it will create,
Its progeny may need to educate !
But 'tis too bad to tax an Empire's purse
To propagate such dogmas—Ireland's curse—
Thro' an unprincipled, unenglish band,
Whose cowardice lets treason rule the land,
And spread thro' ev'ry clime, at Britain's cost,
The sbirri of the Pope, a Jesuit host !
From such mad patronage, what profit springs ?
Who hornets hive, must only gather stings !
These teach Columbia democratic views,
Thro' the confessional, by men like *Hughes*,
Helots of Rome, and branded to maintain
King Pio Nono, and uphold his reign :

Who, by the protean, Papal logic scheme,
Make opposites in politics their game !
Who ape Republic feelings in the west,
While, tools of Autocrats, they crush the east !

Whoe'er is subject to the Roman See,
Can only but to Rome bring fealty !
And trusting men, ungenial to the realm,
To take the conduct of our English helm,
Is but engendering to civil storm,
And calls for revolution to reform ;
As Papal democrat, or subject Greek—
Whate'er the government—must ever seek
His church's rule, for which with zeal he waits,
And Protestant dominion doubly hates !
To one alone, is his allegiance trac'd,
And that his mitred king—the Roman beast—
Whose throne he would exalt o'er land and sea,
While kings, as thralls, his mandates should obey,
As Peter's heir, who when he left his oar,
And boat, and fishing tackle, on the shore,
To take a shepherd's duties, with the crook,
He the tiara too and sceptre took,

The Popedom, by which title it appears,
He's King to kill, and but as shepherd, shears!
And ever in these surging waves of strife—
The swells of cleric and politic life—
Are lash'd to notoriety the foam,
That rides the destinies of France and Rome,
The two great bubbles that attention draw,
The crowns of Peter and the " *coup-d'etat* ;"
And truth and peace, these restless seething pow'rs,
Conspire to banish from these isles of ours!

No CECILS, Britain, now thy councils lead,
Nor STILLINGFLEETS, nor USHERS guard thy creed—
The one some continental influence sways,
And this some Philpot-Wilberforce betrays ;
Our polity to German interests prone,
While Oxford harlequins our pray'rs intone,
With convent governess, some French grisette,
And Jesuit tutors, trior, or quartette ;
Who preach or chant from pulpit, choir, or stall,
With LIDDEL's taste and faith, androginal !
By Papal Pusey—chrysalis transitions,
Producing double Papists for its missions !

Thro' the French idiom, now so much in vogue,
That Paddy's curate daughters doff their brogue,
With England's sinon ministry to vie,
To lisp in French the Virgin's rosary ;
Aiding the schoolmaster—that licens'd gent—
The paid official of the Government !
Of the Commissioner O'Farrel class,
A devotee to Vespers and the Mass ;
Of some lay order, on the church's staff—
And village vendor of some Tel-lie-graph,
The glozing bulletin of papal frauds,
Which treason, perjury, or murder lauds,
When ill for Britain, Irish pegs of hope,
By which to stay some interests of the Pope,
Which counter still to England ever ran,
From Poictiers Legate-spies to friend WISEMAN ;
And still such agents, lackey'd by some T—d,
Subserve this concrete, King-Vicegerent God !
Who thro' such agencies asserts his claim,
By sword and crosier to the World's domain ;
And other monarchs must their cares forego,
To wait upon him, and to kiss his toe !
As mitred viceroy of the prince of air,
Lord of all sov'reigns and St. Peter's chair.

This King of slaves!—tho' destitute of might,
Or even a faculty to claim such right—
Issues his mandates in his bifold trade,
And Priests are prompt the helots to brigade,
For raids of onslaught, and Perugia shows
What mercy from such holy fathers flows.

Britain, to action wake! your social grades
And councils alien influence pervades;
A foreign Bishop-King the Priesthood rules,
And seizes on the peasant, thro' your schools,
Which they direct!—tho' you must pay the cost—
What wonder should your peace be tempest toss'd;
While your young magnates, Pusey-taught, inhale
But papal atmosphere, and woo the gale!
A busy priest-train'd sisterhood of ghouls
Hunt round in couples—and their prey are souls!—
The duties in each walk of life assume,
In Workhouse, Hospital, or Lecture room!
In Nursery and Factory they glide,
These minions of the Church, affairs to guide;
Cheer'd on and lackey'd by a dog-faced train
Of corporate bullies, ingress to attain;
'Gainst law and decency, they take the field,
As namby-pamby courtesy may yield;

" They're convent eleves !" give place ! make way !
Sisters of mercy, how ye dog your prey !
And then some *patron* COUNTESS, or her GRACE
Near to the throne—by some deputed place—
Will lend the influence of Her rank to care
And swell the profits of some saint's bazaar !
Got up to tend and teach those kidnapt fry,
Who, were they Protestants, might starve and die,
But when Saint-Vincent-gypsies, or Saint Tool,
Have caught their prey, they're fed and put to school !

Shame on the courtesy that truth can slight,
And yield to wrong, the homage, as to right ;
It is not English, tho' 'tis now a brand
That burns and blights with infamy the land !
English, alas ! too many things bespeak
The blush of shame, to mantle Britain's cheek.

Where so much class ebriety invites
A foreign taste in church and fashion's rites,
Among the social circles to prevail,
The virus soon must taint the public weal ;
And when each family and college chair,
Invites the teachings of the foreigner,

Prudence should hesitate lest we admit
The *polish'd spy*, or licens'd hypocrite :
And surely, less or more is seen each year,
These plague spots spread in Britain's social sphere !

Unstable in their policy and faith,
Some statesmen, in Her interests, act beneath
The dignity Her arms and empire gain'd
By *Waterloo !*—which still should be maintain'd—
And with a Cromwell's vigor, or Nassau,
Still England's veto should have been the Law ;
Nor would *Savoy,* or *Nice,* be left to feel,
One hour, the pressure of the Despot's heel !
But CANNING rests with PITT and JENKINSON,
And England now has only PALMERSTON,
'Midst Mulgrave Peers and timorous colleagues,
Who leave young Italy to French intrigues,
And clogs on Britain's action, hesitate ;
While France and Spain new pow'rs consolidate !
And thro' a tortuous policy, they lend
These aid, their hostile status to extend,
And plant, for future strife, our deadliest foe
In Egypt, Syria, China, Mexico !

Where France, as in Turin and Rome, we leave
All independent action to enslave!
Making the road to French aggression smooth,
The Bright and Cobden theories, to soothe,
Of peace at any price! for which pretext
They'll Malta give, and Gibraltar next!
For toys to still the wayward Nap!— Kind seers !—
As wickets for his play-grounds in Algiers ! ! !
The Saxon spirit, has she bow'd her head:
Or has she rather to Columbia fled,
To guard the Anglo character and tone
From rowdy traits her offspring should disown ?
Where Irish treasons, wed to French parade,
Engender bigotry and gasconade :—
To Anglo-Saxon truth and energies,
As opposite as the antipodes.—

    The Saxon, proud, indomitable, chill,
Tho' slow to act, retains the steadfast will,
Since wed to Norman courtesy and grace—
Now long united—springs the British race !

    The Norman's chival'rous, aggressive mind,
In action bold, and in his tastes refined,
Fus'd happily with Saxon fortitude,
Forms the true Briton !—not to be subdued—

From Gallic boast and self-inflation free ;
The Frenchman's God and soul is Vanity !
Half kin to Irish Celts !—and Erin's boys
Will kiss and box, and laugh, and pout their joys ;
But ever too impulsive for success,
Their quarrels lead, or follow, their caress !
And where the objects much pursuit require,
Too gay to persevere, they soon retire !
Quick, pliant, with a warm impulsive sense,
Too ready to embrace, or take offence :
And, as in action, versatile—in thought,
As ready to forgive your greatest fault ;
Forgetting prudence where the passions move,
And, as in umbrage, fickle too in love ;
Gay, witty, careless in success or sorrow,
Enjoy to day, to live on hope to morrow !
Yet to one feeling fixt—that one indeed
Is the true pivot of their complex creed ;
The nucleus of the gay, elastic heart,
With which they're taught in death they must not part!—
The innate hate of England, which expands
As Britain educates Rome's Jesuit bands ;
From whom for years her church a Priesthood draws,
As the most Protean, to subserve her cause,

Who 're trained with pertinacity untir'd,
To brawl when most they get, for more requir'd.

But the stern Saxon, and his brother Thane,
The Anglo-Norman, is of other mien ;
Offend him, and you never may succeed
To heal the stroke, that may for ever bleed ;
For tho' revenge he proudly may despise,
He'll not permit the wound to cicatrize :
Grav'd as in adamant, the deed is set,
He may forgive, but knows not to forget ;
From his fixed purpose, he will not retreat,
Success alone his ardour can abate ;
To yield he scorns, he knows not how to bend,
A proud repulsive foe, but sterling friend.

And sprung from these, an Irish class we own,
The truest friends of England and her throne,
Who, where their blood has mix'd with Saxon race —
Three-fifths of Ireland's sons we so may trace—
The character as temper'd steel we view,
In polish'd merit, as in action true !
'Tis but where papal influence throws its shade,
That acids blacken, or corrode the blade ;

5

And Britain with such sons—thro' her extent—
Within her Empire is omnipotent ;
But she has bowed to foreign tastes too long ;
In some degree, to insult and to wrong,
While lackey Barons set the crowd agape,
Teaching our Nobles how to bow and scrape ;
To beggar Princes, of outlandish breed,
And future hope of Kings, for England's need,
As Saxon lineage, should not press her throne,
Tho' Princes ere such Highness' names were known ;
And whose descent, thro' lineal honours ran,
From years before the reign of Athelstan !
Some too whose wide demesnes and fair estates
Surpass the realms of German potentates !
Whose Princely revenues, the rank sustains
Of England's Norman Dukes and Saxon Thanes ;
Whose proud escutcheons, dazzling with the rays
Of Britain's battlefields and councils, blaze !
Yet strange to say, a feudal law of pride
To please a fool, such merit sets aside ;
And that his progeny should but espouse
A partner from some bubble foreign house,
With pension from the state, the usual plague
Entail'd on Britain by each German league.

The fruitful source of protocols and jars ;
Of arm'd neutralities and bitter wars !
Hundreds of millions of the public purse
Have fail'd to mitigate this crying curse :
Nor should our senates for a moment brook
Such insult to disgrace their statute book :
That pension'd Kings and Highnesses by dozens
Our taxes should support—they're costly cousins—
Or senate, Army, Navy, Church and Law
Be made to minister to their eclat !

No wonder that a Reuben soubriquet,
In peace and war the Empire should betray,
That still its blood and gold each field should strew,
From Ramilies to deadly Waterloo ;
Playing the Quixote in some thousand fights,
For continental pauper princes' rights.
By German feuds to balance Europe's scale—
As well it might be hoped the sun to veil—
And were our statesmen but to England true,
They'd scout such dreams and German unions too ;
An ape's Utopia, who to Empire led,
Rather esteem'd his paltry German shed—

Where 'mongst his tinsel'd cousins he had birth—
Than prize the noblest diadem of earth!
Of which he never knew the worth—and died
The fatuous devotee of feudal pride!—
Another of his race, too, lost the gem,
The richest of the British diadem;
Child of her language, of her faith and fame,
Columbia!—ever honoured be the name!

But lo! the star of England beams more bright,
To cheer the Empire with a chaster light;
A truly British Princess now is seen,
And Providence anoints VICTORIA Queen!
The homage of each Saxon heart to gain—
Long, happy, and triumphant be her reign.

THE HOMESTEAD.

CANTO THE FOURTH.

HOME ! there is fond enchantment in the word—
For many cares a harmonizing chord ;
And here as if awaking from repose,
Some by-gone years appear a Lethean doze ;
As from my room the flowers and shrubs I see,
Familiar to my care from infancy.

That spreading Beech, inscribed by many a friend,
Where now their names in hieroglyphics blend ;
And there, the poplar bows, with pliant grace,
To ev'ry zephyr, as the lord in place ;
Wooing those hoydens, in their janty dresses—
The gay laburnums, with their golden tresses.

But of those trees, which add to home's delight,
The Apple-tree, most grateful is to sight ;

As 'mongst the maidens stands the lovely bride,
She of the woodland is the graceful pride,
While in the garden, or the gay parterre,
Each border owns the shelter of her care ;
Where profit with her patronage combines,
Humbly domestic, in espalier lines ;
She in the lawn, or woodland, tow'ring high,
Spreads her sweet foliage to the genial sky,
Blushing with health and teeming prospects gay,
Her ev'ry bud is crown'd with a bouquet ;
Pouring rich tides of perfume far and near,
She stands alone, in bloom, without a peer,
With promise of champagne and tempting pie,
To greet the bon-vivant and gourmand's eye ;
Nor less her charms attract the witching fair,
To her ripe offering in the chaste dessert ;
With blushing sun-kiss'd cheeks to hail their glance,
Which vie with cheeks of love and esperance—
Leading desire their mellowness to sip,
And steal the soul's enchantress to the lip !—
What wonder that her tempting fruit gave rise,
To thoughts of trespass e'en in paradise ;
Alas ! that she, creation's crowning ray,
Whom wondering seraph crowded to survey ;

With matchless beauty grac'd, and witching pow'r,
Bowed to the wishes of that tempting hour ;
God's only daughter, dazzling from his hand,
Inspiring love, then pure as his command ;
Whose breath gave fragrance, and her lips the hue,
To ev'ry fruit and flow'r she pressed them to,
And which, decades of centuries of decay,
Have not extinguish'd to the present day.

'Twas Adam's part to name the bird and beast,
And Eve's, as more alive to grace and taste,
Each paradisian shrub, or plant or tree,
Designed for odour, fruit, and symmetry ;
And as she named and kiss'd the fruit or flower,
It took its tints and perfume, as her dow'r :

Not all were favour'd—that were out of place—
She told off some as foils, the rest for grace—
Those disappointment paled, but while they bent,
She breathed upon them, and some odour lent,
While other some, which flaunted in gay dress,
To claim her note, she doom'd to biliousness !

Alas ! how faded now, and scatter'd wide,
The flow'rs and fruits that paradise supplied ;

Now only mantled in some patchwork robe,
Pining and lingering on our smitten globe;
Ah! where's expression, or the mind to frame
Conceptions, to elucidate the theme?
Not poesy, nor language makes pretence
To trace the scene as tangible to sense;
In visionary hours is only giv'n
A misty glance—and visions are from heav'n—
When Earth's first summer spread her ev'ry gem,
For Eve to wreath her nuptial diadem;
With fruits and flow'rs her every wish to meet,
And strew the footprints of her bounding feet.

Ah! who may name the buds and blossoms now,
From which she cull'd to deck her angel brow;
And form the chaplet to adorn her hair,
With angels waiting on the happy fair;
Yet from some traits of that now-drooping host,
The apple's bloom, and rose, recal the most;
But chief, perhaps, the rose, above the rest,
Seems to retain attractions from her breast;
Her lips vermilion, and th' exhaling traits,
That breath of paradise alone conveys;
And still as then it holds the foremost place,
The first in perfume, as the first in grace.

And as I gaze upon their trellis'd stems,
Blushing with dew-bath'd, drooping, odorous gems,
Some incidents of boy-hood light the past
From mem'ry's niche, where glimmering still they last.

Here too in converse with herself, alone,
Amongst these shrubs and flow'rs she deems her own,
Her dual notes the cuckoo iterates—
That mockingly the school-boy pert repeats—
Whose song, monotonous to hope gives rise
Of fruitful summer, and of sunny skies;
And by the village hinds her first essay,
With joy is hail'd—a welcome holiday!
Incessantly she chants while May inspires,
But grows more chary when the spring retires:
Then, half domestic, thro' the lawn she flits,
Musing, or musical, in playful fits.

But more domestic, I may not forget,
The friend of man!—that universal pet,
Whose social warblings soothes the humblest lot,
And rather than the palace, courts the cot!
The Robin-red-breast, confident while shy,
Cautious of capture, yet for ever nigh,

How often on my lonely steps he hung
In midnight's solitude, and sweetly sung
In Bruno's shades, the haunt of fairy troops,
While angling there among their festive groups,
In the high noon of night, those favorite streams,
While the wrapt villagers lay bound in dreams;
The Robin, wakeful, warbled at my feet,
His melody of night-song, softly sweet;
And while his notes and pathos won my ear
I felt some guardian spirit too was near!

How sweet at early morn the lawn to tread,
And own the cheering gifts by nature spread,
Or rather, what His bounteous hands display,—
Whom earth, and air, and seas, and plants obey;
With every creature in the complex plan,
Man, only man excepted, ingrate man,
Who, in his pride, oft labours to destroy,
Or mar the blessings which he might enjoy,
And, in the cecity of moral night,
Sleeps on, or gropes unconscious of the light.

Hail, thou, my soul, the freshness of the lawn,
In all the shadings of advancing dawn;

As steal the rays of May's enchanting morn,
How rich the breathings of the *plumy* thorn ;
Whose tufted sprays with teeming odours rise,
And waft a joyous homage to the skies ;
Of various choirs ! the tiny and the great—
To claim the notice of a faithful mate :
In tuneful truth they publish from each spray,
Life without love is but a sunless May ;
A doctrine, which as countless years evolve,
Eternity to man may only solve,
Thro' which, 'tis life to love ; this life be mine,
This emanation of the love divine ;
That owns not, glows not, in another flame,
While life, thro' love, expands in the Supreme.

   Earth's earliest love, as sacred records tell,
Was a divided one ; so Adam fell ;
And duty, innocence, and life unpriz'd,
Rather than part his Eve, he sacrificed ;
As freedom too, that gem of earthly bliss,
A Jacob bartered for a Rachel's kiss ;
But those young days, no doubt, required such plea,
A mate to soothe the loss of liberty ;
Greece then, nor Roman feats, had lit no page,
Nor had they books, perhaps, in this good age,

Save the Welsh annals, or Milesian rolls,
Recording Paddy's fights, and Fion M'Coul's,
Some centuries—we need not be precise,
Ere Adam got his lease of paradise.

Not empire's fame, nor patriot's feelings then,
Swelled to proud chivalry the souls of men ;
When all the blessings which to life gave charms,
Was held within the circle of the arms,
And flocks and herds were but the nomad's care,
His flow'rs and fruits he gather'd every where ;

No villa then his taste or pride requir'd,
To make him either envied, or admir'd,
Nor parks nor gardens needed ; (these arose
In after years, those Chatsworths and Leasoes ;)
In miniature, or on that princely scale,
Peculiar to our English commonweal :
Where elegance of taste with comfort's charm,
Surround the manor, and the homestead farm.

Tho' Hampton's, Greenwich, Warwick's noble chase,
With some few more, have gain'd a lasting place
In mem'ry's niche—my native parks the while
Recall me back to dreams more juvenile,
As o'er the scene imagination wings,
And each priz'd object observation brings.

And here the village spire attracts my gaze,
Reviving memories of by-gone days,
As to its church my willing footsteps sped,
To join my class, of which a boy stood head ;
The youngest there, but, ardent to succeed,
The little catechumen kept the lead ;
To all was manifest his prompt replies,
As still he ever won the envied prize ;
He knew me then, but very few beside,
He mix'd not in their plays, they said, thro' pride ;
Perhaps it was, yet in whatever mood,
With me he'd read, or walk thro' park and wood ;
Playful, but ever haughty was his brow,
I knew him then, he scarcely knows me now.

How chang'd the scene, in but few flitting years,
The Pastor dead, and scattered those compeers,
Some sleep, and some to distant lands have flown,
And in his seat, he worships now alone !

Where, once attentive, all were wont to hear,
A listless few, too careless, now appear :
In pews half empty, where so late the crowd,
To hear the words of life, in rev'rence bow'd,
Tranc'd in the witching melodies of praise,
The Pastor's family were prompt to raise ;

While worshippers participating hung,
Rapt in the heavenly harmonies they sung !
And where the most fastidious ear was won,
Now brawl and dissonance the senses stun !

But change of Pastors led to change of taste ;
Now village-gossip agents chime the feast ;
Screen'd in some office, or mechanic's shed,
The taste by other pabula is fed,
Than psalms, or visiting the peasant's bed.

The good M'Clin—k's rectory and place
Witness not now his suavity and grace :
Call'd from his labors to his crown of bliss,
The poor their friend and watchful teacher miss ;
While Rome for his successor well may cheer !—
From whose address her faith has nought to fear.

Where with religion rank unites, we see
Some types of humble, active ministry ;
Where other teachers, sprung from lowly life,
Aspire to gain but status and a wife :
And sensitively cautious, such are sure
To slight their natal class and kindred poor ;
In their professional and hireling trade,
To ape a genteel rank in masquerade !

Assuming to perform a cleric part,
Too many try to play with small desert ;
And in the flowing toga and black coat
Keep from all kindred intercourse remote !
While Punch's symmetry and leering knack
Lead some to grimace when behind your back,
And shrug the shoulders, or the eyelids raise
Where brother ministers were nam'd with praise ;
Protrude the tongue, or thumb the nose aside
Unseen, to intimate the speaker lie'd ;
But promptly cut his stick, and take French leave,
Presto, without good-bye, should you perceive ;
And characters like this should never be
Entrusted with the Gospel ministry :
As where such gifts and habitudes combine,
The talented possessors only shine
As lepid mimes, who with low gossip aims
Hang on the rich, with tattle for their dames ;
And from the pulpit hope for less renown,
While such deserts are trammel'd by the gown.

Poor are the prospects where such men appear,
To lead, or aid a cause as volunteer :
An Evangelic part to act, or try,
Is farcical indeed, and truth must sigh ;

As ev'ry platform sinks, when there we see,
Moral, or physical deformity,
Feeling at ease, while they adjust their brass
As gold !—'tis yellow, and with some 'twill pass—
With the bold merit, 'tis their sole pretence,
Of an impassive, meddling impudence.

   Nor here must our remarks be deem'd unkind,
Not private life for notice is designed,
And charity itself may be severe
On public men, when follies taint their sphere,
And ministers, as such, we must not spare :
Careless of obloquy, the Muse to truth
Clings with devoted love, as fix'd as Ruth ;
And with the sterling object, to correct
The putid foibles, friendship can't protect,
Yet sadly feels the character, as shewn,
Is true to life, and to the Muse well known.

   Nor shall we here permit the Muse to pass
The claims of London's fam'd Saint Barnabas,
Where we have mark'd the antics of its ass !
With other cleric help-mates there, who pray
In unison with *Liddel's* papal bray :
Where in the farce the capers of the donkey,
Were imitated by each curate monkey !

And worthy too of note our meed we bring
To *Liddel's* juggling brother—*Bryan King*—
He who exhibits in Saint George's fields,
Whose merits, to no other Pusey yields,
As *Lid*——l's rival and his *pugs*, and seeks
To beat them out in playing popish freaks;
And comic as his cousin Brien O'Lin,
He in the church calls forth the laughter din,
By somersaults to Rome! and his acclaim
Is only second to a *Liddel's* fame,
As emulous of praise from the red hat,
In ceremonials each the Acrobat!—

And such men preach, and hold preferment high,
To whom we must all confidence deny;
Who take a parson's calling, to pursue
A trade to live by, but its faith undo!
Who thro' a patronage we must deplore,
Eat as a gangrene in the Church's core,
Repudiate the BIBLE and its truth,
By propagating dogmas of Maynooth;
Leading the church to Rome, by state gradations,
Professors, parsons, prelates, convocations;
A Pusey, Philpot Liddel, cleric train
In state concatenation's golden chain!

6

And where religion merges in a trade,
Just teaching how to spout a hebdemade ;
To live by vending theologic slop,
Making the house of God its sabbath shop ;
Under the license of that motley set,
A Papal-pusey-atheist cabinet !
Ah ! where religion to such state is tied,
The Devil and the Pope the spoils divide.

The Gospel's interests are too dear to me,
To tolerate the vile duplicity
Of those who seek its life-fraught gifts to spread,
As a profession but to gain their bread ;
Who'd tune to mass, or muezzins, their fiddles,
The rival mountebanks of *Kings* or *Liddels.*

Some Tory monks, as parsons, thus are found,
Their trade of papal rituals to propound ;
Yet tho' such Philpot-spawn the mass may mew,
Thank God we've TAITS, and STOWELLS, not a few,
Whose hearts and lips the Altar's living coals
Have warm'd and sanctified, for care of souls ;
On whom the high necessity is laid,
And who in converts seek their labours paid !
Call'd to these duties, they embrace the cross,
And worldly speculations treat as dross !

These men I prize, and feel the antipast
Of love, for such, that shall for ever last.

Drawn to the church—as I observed its spire—
Which love of truth still leads me to admire ;
I feel the dangers that religion wait,
As now connected with a pie-bald State.
When first I worshipp'd there, truth held the helm,
And God's protection crown'd the British realm !
When VICT'RY *Marshall'd* her for WATERLOO,
No perjur'd senators her councils knew,
Nor round her neck was thrown the Helot chain,
That binds the nations in the harlot's reign :
The monster-mother-spouse, who daily broods
A million deities !—her wafer gods !
And now the SEES of England dares dispense ;
Muse ! 'tis a *sombre* prospect—lead me hence.—

Muse, lead me hence, to yonder pine-clad height,
Kerrhill, whose paths of shade, my steps invite,
To tread its hanging verge, and in mid air,
Enjoy the landscape from the lady's chair—
Upon its promontory brow—a seat,
Far above lawns and woods, beneath our feet,

Thro' which the Slaney, flowing gently, steals,
While wide spread oaks and beech its beauty veils;
And ever kiss the dimples which they shade,
Before the current gains the open mead.

How beautiful appears the shelter'd chase,
Between the river and the hill's green base,
Rising precipitous, while sombre pines,
Its swelling, convex, prominence defines.
And noble oaks, and elm, and flow'ring thorns,
Like guardian sentinels, the glade adorns;
With the dark chesnut, that so proudly tow'rs,
A grateful shade—a pyramid of flow'rs!

And flaunting in the breeze, full drap'd in green,
Or purple robes, the beech is gayly seen
To grace the lawn, and emulous compete
To hold in rank the secondary state,
As next the oak, so beech and sycamine,
In landscape merit, claim a noting line :
But chief the beech so varied in its hue,
Attractive still in storm, or calm, we view ;
Whose portly oval symmetry and height,
And pliant branches waving with delight,
Dance wanton in the gale, and toss their arms
In the elastic grace of nature's charms :

Or placid in the calm, their fronds repose
In the rich mantles bounteous May bestows !
While numerous buds put forth their tiny vines,
In pensile growth, which hang like silken twines,
With downy leaves, as summer gives them strength,
Rise to extend the branches' drooping length ;
As to salute the grassy turf they try,
The leafy boughs a hanging tent supply ;
As from the trunk, projects the rural shed—
The ample penthouse nature's care has spread:
A shelter from the summer's sudden show'r,
When clouds too overcharg'd their gatherings pour ;
And from the mid-day's sun-subduing heat—
A grateful refuge and secure retreat.

    Bounding the view, not too remote nor near,
Mount Leinster's group, in massive files appear,
Mantled in purple heath—imperial dye—
King of the landscapes that around him lie ! ·
And at our feet the dell of Bruno spreads
Its fairy lawn, a miniature of meads,
On all sides shelter'd by the lordly oak ;
And smiling peaceful in its warrior cloak,
While sure defence is ever nigh to aid,
As England's lion couching in its shade.

I prize the oak and love his leafy mound,
The sheltering monarch of the vales around,
Lord of the forests of the north and west—
He to the cedar's sway resigns the east,
Content with Europe's and Columbia's throne;
He envies not the Crown of Lebanon,
But proudly reigns as when he threw his shade
Around his Barons upon Runnymede,
Whose chivalry, nor Prince nor Pope could draw
To foist *a foreign code* in England's law!
The manly veto of their MERTON vote,
Rome's priest-enslaving policy first smote.
Those hearts of oak, who sturdy as the tree,
Inscrib'd his every leaf with liberty!
Wreathing his merits with historic thought,
And his achievements too, where NELSON fought!
Bearing the thunders, and the lightning's blaze,
Of battle, round each coast to distant seas,
'Till ev'ry wave was crested with the fame
Of England's might, and NELSON'S glorious name!
Rais'd by the providence of GOD to save,
The Isles of Britain from the drenching wave,
Which saturated Europe's plains with gore!
That e'en to Afric's sands the torrent bore;

And stain'd—oh! shame—the matricidal brand,
Plac'd by Columbia in a Mad'son's hand,
To smite the language, liberties, and race,
From which she sprung—and for an end so base—
Leading his country harness'd for the war,
A donkey feat, to drag a despot's car!
An upstart menial, and whose only plea
Was, that he envied England's sov'reignty;
And made of Madison a stepping stone,
O'er slaughter'd millions' blood, to reach his own!
Shaming democracy, 'till men, more true,
Their country from the *Corsican* withdrew,
And his mad worshippers, and cut the chains
That drew AMERICA to deeds like Cain's!
Their mother-land, and brothers to strike down—
That a Bezonian might take Europe's crown.
Ah no! AMERICA, you can't allow
That Empire's wreath should fall from Britain's brow!

By name, by language, and paternal line,
Her poets, statesmen, orators are thine!
And all that soul, or thought, or mind enlists,
Divines, philosophers, and mechanists,
And heroes too—but here combin'd in one,
Statesman and hero, yours is WASHINGTON.

The ALFRED of Columbia, Alfred's peer,
Hero and statesman, patriot, and seer !
Nor less those glorious feats on fields of blood,
You claim their fame as yours—and so you should—
From CRESSY as POICTIERS, and AGINCOURT,
To WATERLOO, as well as hundreds more,
Where England's Saxon princes and your sires,
Whose blood, American desert, inspires—
Those Gallic laurels won, their sons retain,
Your heirloom too—of which you may be vain !—

    Your brothers' triumphs, as your fathers'—shed,
A brilliant halo, worthy of your head !
Co-heirs in fame, the captains are your own,
Down to the present age of WELLINGTON ;
And up to CHURCHILL, as the line you trace,
'Tis yours to glory in your Saxon race !
And MARLBRO's fame which Britain's bosom warms,
Consummate in diplomacy, and arms,
The prince of captains—without rival yet,
In fields of contest, or the cabinet !

    Tho' CHURCHILL's name shall English combats plume,
'Till time itself the Empire shall entomb !
A titled snarler rais'd by party heat,
His character would fain assassinate !

And in the pique and meanness of a clan,
Would stab his country's honour in the man :
But ALLISON deprived him of his skean,
To leave him sweltering in his little spleen !
With those who dare to shade what honor lights,
Such politicians as some cotton knights,
Who chivalry despise ! and England's home
For ought they care, become a fief of Rome,
Or French department—e'en the Muscovite
Might seize it, unoppos'd by men like Bri—t
And C——n ! who more prize a cotton rag,
Than all the triumphs of the Red-cross-Flag !
And rather aliens aid, and side with those
Who rail at Britain and applaud her foes !
And in their wanton charities of heart,
Admire the mercies of friend Buonaparte,
And scarce find terms to spout theircreed's eclat
For the dear Moloch of the *coup d'etat*
Whose sacrifice, by fusillades invite
The plaudits of the patriot school of Bright !
Whose polity is seldom to be found
On the contracted field of British ground.
Utilitarian on his broad-brim plan—
And much too little of the Englishman—

Supporting parties ramified in sect,
Where English feeling never meets respect ;
Whose dolt-O'Noodle-Officers brigade,
To curse her faith, her language, or her trade !
The serfs of Rome, whose daily supplication,
Weary their saints for England's degradation ;
For which, their very souls they'd jeopardize ; —
In the vain hope their Church to aggrandize—
With pæans to the Beast, the feat parade,
And rosaries to their newest goddess made !

But till America shall also wane
Before the papal cross, as abject Spain,
And Saxon manhood lose its mind and nerve,
Rome may her hopes and jubilants reserve,
Nor hail the chaste vaticinating dreams,
That lend afflatus to McC——y's themes
Of exhum'd London, usher'd into day,
From buried ages, as was *Nineveh*,
To please those Celts—as Mac himself ideal—
Whose aspirations wish his visions real ;
But then the taste that Marlbro' could decry,
May tomb his country too in fantasy,
And such Pythonics may enchant the Gael,
Who Britain curse, as C——l and McH——le,

Whose flocks to nurture in their hate they strive,
And only on such pabula they thrive,
While the clan-ravings English Macs thus vent,
Supply to Paddy's feast, the condiment!

But not such morbid sentiments be mine,
The Muse, another future can divine;
Nor Celtic pike, nor stake, nor faggots' pile,
Tho' blessed by Rome, shall desolate the Isle!

And tho' class pride and party-feuds may aid,
With papal rites the empire to degrade
To premature senility, and hand
To paralytic influence, the land,
Yet England's genius shall preserve her name,
And institutions *in Columbia's fame !*
Her eldest born—and empire in her race,
O'er ev'ry land, thro' time, the world to grace!—
Yes, ever as her sons recal their sires,
And Anglo-Saxon worth their bosom fires,
Lit by the study of the rich archives,
And records where their fathers' merit lives!
The men who fought and bled in honor's cause,
Contending for their country's faith and laws!
Nor battle, stake, or scaffold, stayed their zeal,
'Till they establish'd freedom's Commonweal,

Which traitors to such worth too lightly prize,
And by their vanity may compromise.

Yet tho' the dear old fatherland may bow,
And puppy minions disregard it now ;
As *Pusey tastes*, and *jugglery* obtain,
To sap the faith, on which its interests lean ;
Columbian statesmen from such influence freed,
Shall guard their father's idiom and their creed ;
Which no class privilege, or money test,
From their descendant kindred e'er shall wrest,
Nor tutor'd, nor by governesses taught,
To worship gingerbread, or Juggernaut.

Her stripes, and stars, shall distant regions cheer,
Guarding the faith, wherever they appear,
From west to east, and Britain's language spread,
Till the last trump shall wake the sleeping dead ;
'While Anglo-Saxon anthems shall arise,
From every land, and close earth's obsequies !

OCCASIONAL POEMS.

OCCASIONAL POEMS.

EMAN AC KNUCK, OR NED OF THE HILLS.

It is assumed that this outlawed Prince was betrothed to the Princess Eva, daughter of the Irish Monarch Dermot M'Morough, when the Saxons landed in Ireland, and learning that she looked with admiring eyes on Strongbow, their chief, I suppose " Eman ac Knuck " as under her casement making this last midnight appeal to her love, for the subject of those verses.

WHILE cares, dear Eva, banish sleep,
   I steal to thee—to pay my vows—
Thro' foes who murderous vigils keep,
   While night-dews chill my weary brows !
The hills, by day my lone retreat,
   The crag, my only couch of rest,
While foreign hearts to revels beat,
   For thee and Erin throbs my breast !

To free our much-lov'd home and lands,
  Your cheers once edged my daring sword,
To battle with their bravest bands
  And their most proud, invading lord !
Can you become that Leader's wife ?
  The thought to me, than death, is more !
And the sad day shall close my life,
  In sacrifice of Saxon gore !—

Eva, who hearken'd from above,
  While Eman's murmurs claim'd her ear,
Without responding to his love—
  Oh ! fly, she cried, nor linger here,
My father aids your noble foes,
  They seek for you, oh ! quickly flee !—
Your country's hopes on you repose—
  And, Edmund, lose no thought on me !

Farewell then, Eva, I'll obey ;
  My country more than love I prize,
And fate may, with some brighter day,
  Illume the path she now denies !—
Till then let strangers tread my halls,
  To lose thee is the greater ill,
And, Eva ! while my country calls,
  I'll live for love, and vengeance still !

And Eman to the Hills retir'd ;

   From Eva now he hope had none ;

For she the Saxon chief admir'd,

   And soon her hand and heart he won !—

And Edmund's Halls and fair demesne,

With Leinster too, became her dow'r—

And Eva's union with the Thane

   Gave Erin up to British pow'r !—

And still the Saxon onward prest,

   'Till Erin's ev'ry stay was gone ;

And only gave the falchion rest,

   When she became with England one !

For Erin's cause with Eman fell,

   Tho' still his deeds her Bards inspire !—

And proudly patriot bosoms swell,

   As to his fame they tune the Lyre !

7

SONG.

Written for a social dinner party, where many of different politics and creeds were invited to meet at a hospitable friend's table.

AIR :—"*Patrick's Day.*"

WHEN friendship and wit at the board are presiding,
　To breathe on the bosom, as summer on snow,
How worthless the heart, that in bigotry biding,
　Refuses to melt in their kindly glow—
To wine and good humour, each prejudice bending,
　No party concerns should ruffle the soul—
　　　But all our employment,
　　　Be social enjoyment,
While spirit and spirit in harmony blending,
　United should hallow the feast of the bowl !
　　　O ! then let it, who shall
　　　Be 'mongst us most social,
And each for the palm be contending.—

Life, like the vessel becalm'd on the ocean,
　When spirits, our life-sails, in languishment droop,
We drift with time's current, the moment's emotion,
　Which bears us away from the track of hope ;

But if a gale rises, her gay sails distending,
    She brings up her course on the wings of the wind—
        Thus we, when we're pleasant
        In gusts like the present,
With mirth for our pilot, and wine-tides befriending,
    Leave years of despondence far distant behind—
                O ! then let it, who shall, &c. &c.

Then hail the gay moments, which beam o'er chill sorrow ,
    Like meteors that flash on the north's dreary night,
Illuming each vista of hope, 'till the 'morrow
    Of light and true liberty cheer our sight,
When pride now, the ties of humanity rending,
    No longer for prey may enshackle each land ;
        But brother and brother,
        Embracing each other,
The despot and bigot shall chase from offending,
    And only for freedom and truth draw their Brand ;
        'Till then let it, who shall
        Be 'mongst us most social,
And each for the palm be contending.

When first I met Kathleen, I felt such a thrill
Pervade ev'ry pulse, that I sigh'd as if ill ;
And yet so bewitching to sense was the smart,
I foster'd the feelings that seized on my heart.
'Till then to some Belles, whether brunette or fair,
I sang, and made love, with a heart free from care—
But Kathleen's blue eyes on my bosom did beam,
And quicken'd a throbbing to wake at her name !

The page of my country, more early imprest,
The fire of ambition to light in my breast,
And lead me to death fields, with heroes to share,
In culling the laurels of glory to wear !
But now other prospects my bosom did sway,
And love was the captain I chose to obey—   .
While Kate threw around me enchantments so sweet,
That all my ambition I laid at her feet.

When glory had faded 'fore Kathleen's bright eyes,
I found her too vain to be pleased with one prize,
And somewhat afraid I'd be left in the lurch,
I took to my beads and a zeal for the church !

'Twixt love and devotion my peace was so torn,
I curs'd the sad moment in which I was born—
'Till the blood of the grape drew my penchant from wars,
And I smother'd my love and my zeal with cigars.

Devotion and glory are themes of romance,
For Priests and their puppets in Britain and France ;
And ladies and quidnuncs may bow to each joke,
While life's richest treasures are brandy and smoke !
As the dear lit cigar ! O what eyes half so bright ?
What lips half so sweet, as the wassail at night ?
And true bucks quit those objects of vulgar pursuit,
To soothe all life's cares in thick clouds of CHEROOT !

SONG.

"THE EMIGRANT'S FAREWELL TO ERIN."

AIR :—" *Cean du deelish.*"

ERIN dear, tho' fate may sever
   Ev'ry tie that holds me thine,
Fond remembrance shall for ever
   Round my heart thy love entwine !
Other climes may boast more treasures,
Fairer skies and gayer pleasures,

More of friendships, ardent, willing
To warm a heart with sadness chilling!
　　Yet, while such prospects glow,
　　O'er thee my tears must flow—
　　　　Erin, adieu!—
Tho' fortune my life-bark may steer with acclaim,
Each bright wave of pleasure shall swell at thy name,
　　　　Dear Erin, when far—far from you.

Tho' each hope you gave has faded,
　　Like those flow'rs that strew the tomb;
Spells, by sweet affection wreathed,
　　O'er their mem'ry shed perfume!
Fare thee well!—tho' treason's riot
Lords it o'er thy homes and quiet!
Soon shall patriot spirit beaming
Lead thee from the traitor's scheming;
　　　　But e'er you greet that day,
　　　　I shall be far away,
　　　　Far from thy cheer:
Yet hailing the time when your day-star will rise,
And light and pure liberty gladden your skies,
　　　　I welcome the hope with a tear.

While bright visions flit before me,
　　Of thy future calm repose,
Soft regrets in tides steal o'er me,
　　Far from thee my life will close !
Fair Columbia's soil invites me,
Thither fortune too incites me,
Where the star-deck'd flag appearing,
Shades each home with rest endearing ;
　　　Yet, with gay hopes in view,
　　　Sad is my last adieu,
　　　　Erin, we part !
Dear Isle of my birth, where my sires sleep in peace,
No time from my mem'ry thy love may efface,
　　　O Erin, thou home of my heart.

Rockfield, Sept., 1*st,* 1832.

ON THE LEGISLATIVE UNION OF ENGLAND AND IRELAND.

Dark, dark were the motives when traitors conspiring,
    The genius of Erin they sought to entoil—
While peace spread her wings, and far distant retiring,
    Left discord to rule o'er her bountiful soil !
Then bigotry rearing the Banners of slaughter,
To 'stablish the tenets that aliens had taught her;
Shed blood o'er the Island in torrents as water,
    And hallooed the demons of murder and spoil !

Ah ! hapless, indeed, was her state while redeeming,
    She stoop'd, and extinguished her liberties' flame ;
Her birthright as Esau then lightly esteeming,
    She gave to a rival the charge of her fame.—
Oh ! curs'd be the Zealots, who helots fomenting,
Left Erin alone but the choice of preventing
Their schemes of destruction, by sadly assenting
    To raze from the records of Nations her name !

How deeply must grief with affection be blending,
    When she, as the Pelican, pierced her own breast ;
Regardless of self, when the Empire befriending,
    She bow'd to a fate which these evils represt !—

The treasons of Party which long did confound her—
To welcome the beamings that hope flung around her,
And rise to new life from the trammels that bound her,
  To share in the Union—a sceptre of rest!

ON THE GOSPEL'S HOPE FOR ERIN.

O ERIN, my country, tho' long overcast,
The light of thy glory is dawning at last;
Tho' party to drown thee their mad waves did fling,
The dove, with the olive, is now on her wing.

Tho' long o'er the wild surge thy lone bark did ride,
No beacon to cheer thee, no pilot to guide;
The billows subsiding where late you did cope,
At length leave thee safe in the haven of hope—

Yet thy deserts shall blossom and breathe as the rose,
While the lamb and the wolf in the shade shall repose;
The prospects are cheering, thy discords shall cease,
And thy Genius long wilder'd shall hence rest in peace.

LINES

On the American Democratic taste in sending a frigate
to Saint Helena, to convey a stone from the grave of
Buonaparte, as an ornament for the Monument being erected to
WASHINGTON !

" FROM the sublime to the ridiculous
   Is but a step," some Yankees late have shown,
That admix brood of Irish-French—pediculous—
   Who chiefly are for relic worship known,
     And pilgrimage to shrines !—they drag a stone
From Buonaparte's grave, with *Pat*-riot aim,
   To gem the tomb of glorious Washington !
And, with a despot's murders mete *his* fame !—
Blush, Liberty! his very bust might mantled be with shame!

To a foul empty pit, for rubble earth,
   A brig of war was sent, some trash to bring,
A spawn of monkey taste !—for such a birth,
   From intellect or manhood could not spring !
   Nap's only merit was to mould a king
From various low-born clods of his vain line,
   And round the necks of plunder'd States to fling
Chains, to enslave the Tagus, Dnieper, Rhine,
Drunk with each sacrifice of blood, as if with wine !

One ABOUT, monostropic chiel of France,

    A missal-book-Munchausen lately wrote

As history, Yankee Celt-born cliques to trance,

      Where they may martyr'd names for worship note,

      Whom British puissance unhallow'd smote ;

Where Big Napoleon, idol of his praise,

    Heads the French-Haynau list!—too long to quote—

Mixt up with Lannes, Durocs, Junots, and Neys,

'Mongst whom a Washington emits but rushlight rays.

And long has Young America been school'd,

    In spurious maudlin gratitude to sing

Of Gallic aid !—and still this cant is pul'd—

      Tho' France but help to her own fight did bring,

      And, aided by Columbia's nerve and wing,

Prepar'd, with keen address, her shafts to throw,

      Great Britain's pow'r and pride at once to sting,

That too triumphant rival—Gallia's foe—

England that oft had struck French vanity so low !

Not Connaught hags more grimly tell their beads,

    Nor Mormons mourn the sack of their Nauvoo,

Than mongrel Yankees groan their jer'miades

      O'er the mishap of thundering Waterloo,

Which from his pedestal their Dagon threw,
   For Saint Helena's rats to round him dance,
Leaving such Democrats their whine to mew
    In co. with Gaul, their caterwaul of chance—
    That happy one-string air, to soothe republic France !

The Irish hate of Britain, this French spleen,
   Since Waterloo, which struck the Demon down,
May ape a farce of Freedom !—they but feign—
    While heart and hand they're helots to a crown,
    Crouching before a Pope's or Despot's frown !—
French liberty well mates with Paddy's creed !—
    Both prostrate crawl to tyrants and the gown,
To neither Freedom could intrust her meed ;
They'd pawn it for a sash and feather, or a bead !

Anglo-Americans, note well this band,
   Who masquerade in faith, and freedom mime,
Their impress is a false and foreign brand
    French morals, and that ritual Papal chime,
    Which floats like thistledown throughout your clime,
To seed with weeds the soil they rest upon.
    Oh ! chase them from your halls and schools in time !
Keep free the noble land your sires have won,
Your Pilgrim Fathers' home !—the Land of Washington!

SONG.

Written for some American friends assembled to commemorate the birth-day of WASHINGTON, and which was sung after the toast to his memory was given.
Huron, 22nd Feb.

To WASHINGTON let fame
Emblazon with his name,
The proudest page that history may boast—
And while round freedom's fane
Our yearly cups we drain,
Be WASHINGTON and LIBERTY our toast!

From tyranny and Rome,
Which rul'd their Island home,
Our British sires indignant quit that land,
And with the Pilgrims true,
The Saxon genius flew,
To crown Columbia's Empire with command!

They bid our WASHINGTON
To triumph lead us on,
And free the soil from desposts and from slaves;
And under favouring skies,
The spangled flags did rise,
And brightly shone their stars to ride the waves!

The Empire of the Main,
As Saxons, we'll maintain ;
Nor will we worship despots or "Rome's Host"!
Still burn the sacred fires,
Which led our Pilgrim sires,
While " WASHINGTON and LIBERTY " we toast.

Still let us bless the hour,
When hope of foreign pow'r
Was chas'd away for ever from our coast !
And one in heart—while peace
Our festive boards shall grace !—
Be " WASHINGTON and LIBERTY " our toast !

THE SOLDIER'S PARTING.

How sweet the rose of morning,
  While drooping with the dews of night—
Each pearly drop adorning,
  Fresh odour gives and lustre bright !
And thus the tears at parting,
  Which feelings shed o'er loves' adieu—
Each kindred impulse starting,
  Affection's richest charms renew.

When call'd by despot duty
  On tented fields to bear his part,
And fly from home and beauty,
  How trying to the soldier's heart ;
Tho 'Pride to triumph bears him,
  Love claims the half in Victory's cheers,
To hail the fate that spares him,
  To dry the much-lov'd mourner's tears !

Too oft in glory's shading,
  The drooping gems of love are found ;
And crush'd the flow'rs and fading
  That twine that thorny stay around—
To her whose hopes are blighting,
  How sad the solace of the tear,
Tho' he, who love was lighting,
  Should brightest sink on honor's bier !

But who may speak the rapture,
  That swells with joy each anxious breast ?
When safe from death and capture,
  They meet in love's embraces blest !
When with proud laurels wreathing,
  The myrtle decks the Hero's brows,
And lips of truth are breathing
  The glowing pledge of mutual vows !

LINES

On the avowal of sympathy for Rome by some of our fallen
Nobility.

WHEN Lordly traitors lift the hand,
Inscrib'd with Pio Nono's brand,
'Tis time that England's friends should band,
   To save her faith and law,
The spirit of their sires display,
Who lopt the hopes of Papal sway,
And cast the tools of Rome away,
   And crown'd the brave NASSAU !

Hail, Britain, beacon of the Isles,
Where Truth's fair temple shelter'd smiles,
Since rescued from *Italian wiles*,
   Thy Genius *broke that spell*—
O may the knaves who now combine,
Who plot again the foul design,
To bow thee to their Idol-shrine,
   Be spurn'd as dogs of hell—

To quench the beam that BRITAIN lights,
In vain they hope, tho' France unites
With those who prop up heathen rites—
   In other aid *her* trust.

She looks to HIM, her stay before,
On Cressy's plain and Agincourt,
Who Waterloo made drunk with gore
      To bow her foes in dust !

Secure beneath HIS sheltering wing,
The God of battles, Britons, bring
A grateful homage to your King
      " The God of Hosts"—adore—
For lo ! the day prophetic breaks,
O welcome dawn ! now vengeance wakes !
And Babel to its centre shakes,
      To fall !—to rise no more !

ON THE FLIGHT OF PIO NONO FROM ROME.

EIGHT centuries have nearly fled,
    Since first to Erin's land,
The noble, brave Fitzstephen led
    His gallant Saxon band ;
And firmly planted on our soil
    His standard—and unfurl'd
The red-cross flag of Britain's Isle,
    The envy of the world !
  8

How happy now, our Island home,
    Did she but feel, as then,
Repugnant, that the faith of Rome
    Should blight the souls of men ;
Nor leave its marsh-spawn'd monks to croak,
    And lutulize each spring
Of peace, to blind man to the yoke
    Of their vain, mitred king !

But haply brighter days at length,
    In prospects cheer our eyes,
Th' imposter, shorn of his strength,
    A helpless captive lies,
Within the grasp of villain pow'r,
    And flight, as rest appears
Hopeless !—now all his prospects low'r,
    He sinks 'midst Europe's cheers !

And sure and welcome be the stroke
    That smites imposters low,
His sword and Priest-tiara broke—
    Erin again shall know
True peace, and in the nerve of youth,
    Belnding with Britain's might,
Stand forth in panoply of truth,
    To shield their faith and right !

ON THE ACCESSION OF QUEEN VICTORIA.

GOD save the Queen—Victoria reigns!
 Let sov'reign Princes bow,
While lauding millions raise proud strains,
 And Empires crown her brow—
Our hearts and hopes attend her throne,
 And party now must kneel,
To pay a homage, which alone
 Each breast is proud to feel.

Thro' her another era lights
 The age, and freedom smiles!
Victoria's sway, as one, unites
 Her subjects and her Isles!
The East and West, her sceptre own;
 The North and South, approve;
And justice draws around her throne
 The halo of our love.

Then, hail, most gracious Queen! to thee
 Thy suppliant people sues,
To crush each bloated coterie,
 Who privilege abuse;

While equity controls the Helm,
  Round thee our love shall beam,
True, as the sun that lights thy realm,
  And cherish still thy fame !

May glory's star illume thy way,
  'Till East and West shall blend
With ev'ry Isle to woo thy sway,
  And crown thee as their friend—
That Britain's flag, to catch the breeze,
  May proudly be unfurled,
The standard of the Empire-seas—
  The Ensign of the world !

Hail ! happy hope of pow'r and peace
  Thy diadem to twine—
Unfading, 'till you close your race,
  The brightest of your line,
Be ev'ry heart 'till then your own,
  And 'till you're crown'd above—
May justice consecrate thy throne,
  Victoria ! in our love.

GOODWIN, SON, & NETHERCOTT, Printers, 79, Marlborough-st., Dublin.

www.ingramcontent.com/pod-product-compliance
Lightning Source LLC
Chambersburg PA
CBHW032018010726
47493CB00007B/2463